# The Pochsy Plays

# The Pochsy Plays

KAREN HINES

COACH HOUSE BOOKS

first edition, third printing, August 2008

Published with the assistance of the Canada Council for the Arts and
the Ontario Arts Council. We also acknowledge the Government of
Ontario through the Ontario Book Publishing Tax Credit Program
and the Government of Canada through the Book Publishing Industry
Development Program.

NATIONAL LIBRARY OF CANADA CATALOGUING IN PUBLICATION

Hines, Karen, 1963-
    The Pochsy plays / Karen Hines. – 1st ed.

ISBN 1-55245-134-8 (pbk.)

    I. Title.

PS8615.I44P63 2004          c812'.6          C2004-900982-6

*My parents are scientists. My father is an atmospheric physicist and my mother is a physiologist. Their lives have spanned an amazing period in history: one during which, as students, they could innocently marvel at the endless wonders of the universe and at the world's deepest mysteries of creation – and do so without a concurrent dread that their children might not live out their natural lifespans. This book is dedicated to their youthful and total appreciation of all the planets and the stars and the trees and the water and the animals (including humans).*

*Because, despite my parents' abilities to completely dissect creation, they instilled in me a sense of the ultimate magic of it: that it happened at all to begin with, that we are somehow able to apprehend it, and that, as it turns out, there are delicate physical properties that order the fragile chemistry of creation that we can destroy or preserve, as we choose.*

# Contents

9   Foreword

11  Introduction

17  Note on Performance Style


21  Pochsy's Lips

53  Oh, baby
    (Pochsy's Adventures by the Sea)

87  Citizen Pochsy:
    Head Movements of a Long-Haired Girl


150 The Pochsy Songbook

# Foreword
by Darren O'Donnell

Karen told me Pochsy is an anagram of 'psycho.' She just thought I should know. Like I thought you should know. But is that something we really need to know? As it is, I'm nervous enough in Pochsy's presence. But I pass it on to you so I'm not the only one bearing the weight of the information; there's no doubt about it: that chick is fucking dangerous.

She knows too much. She watches a little too much television, pays a little too much attention to details. It's not good for her health, makes her kind of edgy. Fun to be around, though, a lot of laughs, and can that girl sing! When I hear her belting out those entreaties to God, I have to admit to contemplating suicide out of pure joy.

See what I mean? She's dangerous. And she's always doing that thing where she pretends she's more stupid than she actually is. I find that disconcerting. Once I was hanging out with her and it got so bad I had to throw up. She was very understanding, rubbing my back as I rested my forehead on the toilet bowl. You could say I'm in love with her. But I'm in love with everybody. That's just how she makes me feel.

If they made a Pochsy doll I would buy it. There could be a line of Pochsy clothing and I would be the first to wear it and the first to declare the trend dead; she would understand the necessity of the betrayal, we would still be friends. Or, at least, we would still smile and say hi to each other on the street. I wouldn't be surprised if she became president of the universe. Or if she were convicted of a series of cow mutilations. She's just that kind of girl.

There's a lot happening in that cute little skull. Honestly, I think it's the mercury. Doesn't that make your brain swell? Some days I'll be hanging out with her and I'll get the distinct sense her head is going to explode and I don't know whether to puncture a hole in it to relieve some of the pressure or duck my ass behind some serious cover. It's always a hard call. But I realize I become stronger through the process. And for that I'm grateful to her.

There's a lot about Pochsy I don't know. And that's fine with me. I prefer the mystery. I know it can get the better of my imagination but I have some concerns that my imagination couldn't sustain the truth. I know I'm being paranoid, but better safe than sorry. Once I swear it looked like all her hair had turned into snakes. But I had just stood up and the blood rushing to my feet left me a little light-headed and prone to hallucinations; I'm sure it was nothing.

I dream about Pochsy a lot – just those stupid dreams where I think I'm kissing her and I open my eyes to see I'm kissing myself. I inevitably wake up screaming.

I have faith in her, though. Somehow and I'm not too sure how. Or why. Maybe because I have faith in everybody. Like I said, that's just how she makes me feel. Sometimes I'm tempted to lock her in my basement so that I'm the only one who gets to hang out with her, but I don't think that would be fair to everybody else. We all need a little Pochsy in our lives. Frankly, she's what stops me from going crazy.

# Introduction
by Karen Hines

Now it can be told, I suppose. What would become my ticket as a writer actually began as a good old-fashioned performance crutch.

It was 1992. I had been making a pretty good living for an actor of my age and was then engaged with Toronto's Second City Mainstage, as well as directing the horror clown duo Mump and Smoot. Ungoverned by the rational part of my brain, I let frustration with the former and encouragement from the latter talk me into writing my own solo show. Like many a similar project, it might have died in the writer's block phase, but Smoot (a.k.a. John Turner) made sure I applied widely to Fringe festivals and for grant support. If it wasn't for the fact that those festivals had cashed all my entry-fee cheques – and I had cashed those of the government – I might not have felt sufficiently pressured to finish the job.

The hardest thing for me to overcome was my embarrassment. What narcissism, to think that entire roomsful of people would want to watch me, alone, for an unnatural period of time. What could I possibly tell them that they hadn't already heard? I stared at blank pages for months, then spent a few more writing awful material, until my director, Sandra Balcovske, gently suggested I try writing something good. The first performance was less than three weeks away.

My original premise was to act, allegorically, as Canada, spinning a litany of its problems and challenges. Because it was my first play, though, I thought I should go for something meatier and embody the entire world and all of its woes. I tinkered with this for a while, still unsure of who I was or what I was doing, when Sandra made a crucial suggestion. What if my character, the sad and lonely embodiment of all humanity, were to dress up in pink baby doll pyjamas? I considered this for a while. But nothing clicked until I scribbled an accidental song lyric that summarized this baby doll's attitude. Beseeching God: 'I'll believe in you if you'll believe in me ... but not till then.' Eureka: bigger than God, cute as a button, here was a girl whom audiences might actually tolerate.

Ecce Pochsy.* Titanically vain, confidently beloved. But alone and lonely, almost irredeemably so.

Pochsy's utter self-absorption freed me from my own self-consciousness, allowing me to examine the world (specifically my own country, continent, culture) from its very personification. Pochsy's assumption that everyone is gazing at her with admiration, even envy, became the foundation for a whole system of planetary parallels. And in allegory I discovered a form that sheltered me from the danger of onstage self-revelation, even as I unwittingly took my first real steps toward the expression of my own deepest concerns.

The year before I wrote *Pochsy's Lips* I had studied a performance technique called *bouffon*. I had been inspired by this dark form of clowning, which prescribes the use of bodily affliction in combination with parody to achieve its theatri-political effect, as well as an antagonistic, even hateful relationship between performer and audience. But it also disturbed me. It seemed ill-mannered and ill-advised, not to mention deeply insensitive, for an apparently able-bodied performer like myself to 'use' affliction on stage. Furthermore, why would I want to

---

*Pochsy is pronounced 'Poxy.' Her name references the pox, and is an anagram of 'psycho.' Pochsy was christened by Mike Kennard (a.k.a. Mump) after I described the show's premise and told him I was trying to come up with a character name that was both cute and creepy at the same time.

play hatred against anyone who would be good enough to come and see my show?

Yet I had seen the power of on-stage affliction at work, its knack for making ideas, and especially parody, cut just a little deeper. Having spent three years writing and performing at Second City, I had had the great privilege of studying satire and practicing it, live, onstage. But I confess I had been frustrated by what I saw as the potential of satire being too often blunted by the economic urgencies of entertainment.

I was similarly frustrated, even repelled, by my studies in clowning. They seemed to spawn clown performances (say, my own) that ranged from the obnoxious to the saccharine. But clown visionary Richard Pochinko had planted powerful ideas about what he calls 'the personal clown' – basically an intensely visceral performance entity born from the 'celebration of the extremities and the normalcy of the self.' In further contrast to the *bouffon*, Pochinko taught, the clown must love the audience.

Yet, despite my distaste for these seemingly conflicting performance styles, I was somehow compelled to fuse them. Just as one has a 'personal clown,' I figured, one might also have a 'personal *bouffon*' – not simply a character based on random choice of physical deformity, but rather one inspired from within, based on the aspects of oneself that one is repelled by, or on more external horrors. Thus I settled on a character inspired by a more universal dis-ease, on societal and cultural afflictions (spiritual, psychological, physical) from which no one is immune. The more primal the fear, the more deep-seated the dread, the more 'personal' the *bouffon,* I reasoned ... the funnier the satire. I had to think so; the premiere was now days away.

After rejecting crutches, wheelchairs and straitjackets, I decided that mercury poisoning – both as an affliction and as a crime – would be my driving metaphor. Pochsy would be spared the indignity of unmitigated victimhood. Indeed, her complicity in toxifying herself and her world would become as important as her narcissism. Mercury poisoning also offered the tried-and-true bonus of dementia. Now the metaphorical, allegorical, tragic and comedic possibilities for Pochsy seemed pretty much endless.

Despite best efforts I was still writing on the plane to Florida, and *Pochsy's Lips* was only about sixty per cent 'done' when I hit the boards at the Orlando Fringe. Terrified, I improvised my way through vast stretches of vaguely conceived scenes – and made some radical choices I might have resisted had I had more time and presence of mind. But the very public nature of the final, desperate stages of creation conferred upon *Pochsy's Lips* and its performances an open and direct connection between Pochsy and her audience that became a fundamental aspect of the show. 'Onstage development' (as it became less hysterically defined) would become a significant element in the creation of the next two plays as well.

In the end, Pochsy has become my little Frankenstina, sewn together from the severed body parts of white North American consumer culture. Freed of the baldly autobiographical approach to solo performance, I have found the great pleasure of using details from my own cosmos while remaining comfortably anonymous. And in combination with Pochsy's narcissism (which has proven to be a near-magical trick for both contacting and amusing the audience), Pochsy's afflictions have allowed me to wander into some horrific territory while still keeping the whole thing planted squarely in the realm of comedy.

What I have tried to create with these plays is satire for our times, an entertainment that can simultaneously condemn and celebrate humankind. In the true spirit of the *bouffon*, I hope it is an entertainment which certain corporate warriors might come to see, laugh at, hum along with … only to awaken the next morning and inexplicably hang themselves with their Armani ties.

Meanwhile, in the true spirit of the clown, I hope that the audience, presented with a cruelly comedic mirror of their lives, will find, paradoxically, a momentary reprieve from the need to escape them. Because my ultimate goal is to create, in the laughter that springs from a shared sense of futility, a persistent glimmer of hope.

The Pochsy plays are presented here in the order in which they were produced. However, it might be helpful to know that each was written as a prequel to the last. Please feel free to read them in reverse – my editor and I had a difficult time deciding which way to go with this book.

Also, for what it's worth, *Pochsy's Lips* and *Oh, baby* are presented virtually exactly as they were last performed, around 1996. In contrast, although *Citizen Pochsy* has already toured across the country, it has yet to have its first full production, which, at the time I am writing this, is coming up in a couple of months at One Yellow Rabbit's Big Secret Theatre. Some changes are inevitable, in the making of a piece that depends so much on the presence of the audience for its final shaping and detailing.

In all cases, I have written fairly extensive stage directions. These are included as descriptive, rather than prescriptive, records of what happened in the actual productions of these plays.

# Note on Performance Style
by Karen Hines

'Irony depends upon interpretation; it exists in the tricky, unpredictable space between expression and understanding.' – Linda Hutcheon, *Irony's Edge: The Theory and Politics of Irony*

The most important thing about the performance style of these plays is the direct contact between Pochsy and the audience. Though she NEVER calls upon the audience to actually speak, there is a conversational feel to her dialogue. She often looks directly into the eyes of individual audience members, though never for long enough to provoke any real discomfort.

She also sees and hears the audience. Any sound emanating from them (a sneeze, a laugh, a beeping watch) is potentially fascinating to her, or fodder for her wrath. Though singularly focused on enchanting the crowd, she will veer from course if a distraction is particularly disruptive – perhaps to bless a sneezing audience member, or to politely, unrelentingly, question a late-comer. If a telephone rings, she may invite the owner to answer, and will patiently hold the show until they're done.

If the audience is quietly behaved, she will listen to them even more intently, in more subtle and sensitive ways. She hears their silences, their arms crossing and their laughter, and all are of equal interest to her.

Pochsy is always conscious of doing a show, to the point where she will notice lighting shifts or perhaps seem to will them to happen. In each instance, the artificiality and theatricality of the form are both acknowledged by and thrilling to her.

The performance style is one that evolved over time; the ingredients were added in service to and in tandem with the development of the material. It has been informed primarily and most obviously by the performance principles inherent in *bouffon* and clown as well as Second City–style comedy. However, it also draws heavily on classic principles of voice, movement, and more traditional acting technique, as well as a bit of ballet.

The performance walks a very fine line between innocence and cruelty, sweetness and acidity, darkness and light. It never lingers for long at one extreme or the other; rather, there are, more often, two things going on at once. That is, if Pochsy is describing her loneliness, she is probably smiling. If she is sentimental about a greeting card, there is probably an undercurrent of venom at play. When she prays to God, she is prone to condescension. Pochsy speaks in a wispy, child-like voice, except for brief moments when she chooses to chill the audience out. She moves with great delicacy, except when she is wracked by convulsions. And if she is suffering physically and her elegance is compromised, she will surely point her toes. Opposites and tensions are all-important here, and if anything seems particularly earnest, or heartless, the opposite is almost always true as well.

The opposites at play in the script involve constant checks and balances in performance to maintain the tension between dark and light. Pochsy's constant dis-ease is always masked by the ingenue's line: straight back, softly tilted head, exposed neck, delicately posed 'ballet hands,' and, most importantly, very pretty feet. No matter how ugly, sick, vicious or terrified she can get, though, those less attractive moments are fleeting – so brief the audience should wonder if they saw what they think they saw.

These plays have been a wild challenge to perform, especially given that the performances have so far taken place in over a dozen cities, Canadian and American, northern and southern.

19

Partly because of the allegorical nature of the irony and partly because of the blackness of the comedy – and in some cases because of what is seen as religious blasphemy – a passage of text that might make one audience laugh uproariously can cause another to be disturbed, dismissive or outright hostile. When there is a disconnection between my aim as a writer and the audience's apprehension of that aim, between 'expression and understanding,' it is the performance that can right the wrong by easing off, sharpening up or just taking a moment to let things land.

Pochsy has been described more than once as an 'acquired taste,' and this brand of comedy is definitely not aimed at the faint of heart. Pochsy is both a tragic victim and a manipulator, her 'show' both a cri de coeur and a calculated series of tactics in the execution of a more urgent act. By wrapping the macabre images and disturbing ideas of the text in the shiny packaging of pop culture and escapist diversions, the performance is intended, then, to entertain – to charm, amuse and engage the audience so as to keep everyone existing undeniably in the same room, planted firmly in that 'tricky unpredictable space.'

'What we need is a clown for our times. A clown that gives us a larger sense of God in each of us, that celebrates our humanness, our animalness, and the times we can touch each other in a moment of laughter.'
– Richard Pochinko

'*Bouffons* are the hunchbacks, the lepers, the syphilitics, everything humanity has rejected … but they come to tell us, God's beautiful children, that all aspects of humanity belong to everyone. In the grotesqueness of the *bouffon* is a truth about humanity.'
– Philippe Gaulier

# Pochsy's Lips

*for Brad, for Richard and for Shirl*

## Performance History

*Pochsy's Lips* was first presented by Pochsy Productions at the Orlando Fringe Festival in Orlando, Florida, in April 1992. It then toured to Fringe festivals in Montreal, Saskatoon, Edmonton, Vancouver and Victoria. Pochsy Productions presented a full production at the Poor Alex Theatre in Toronto in November 1992. Subsequent productions were presented at venues in Canada and the US, including the Actors Theatre of Louisville, Dallas Theatre Centre, the Denver International Women's Festival, Alice's Fourth Floor (NYC) and Mixed Blood (Minneapolis).

Pochsy: Karen Hines
The Musician: Greg Morrison

Text, lyrics and melodies by Karen Hines
Directed by and written in collaboration with Sandra Balcovske
Music and sound by Greg Morrison
Original recorded score by David Hines
Set by Campbell Manning
Lighting by Michel Charbonneau

## Set

In the centre of the stage there is an ancient hospital bed with white iron head- and footboards, like from the thirties. There is no mattress, only unpainted wooden slats held together with a thick silver chain. The slats and chain are twisted and warped, and the head- and footboards bend in toward each other. The bed looks horribly uncomfortable, and even dangerous.

An old white rotary dial phone sits on the bed. At the foot of the bed there is a low table covered with reams of cream-coloured surgical gauze for a tablecloth. The gauze drapes onto the floor, sometimes extending in spots, like tentacles. The table is piled high with get-well cards – so many that they spill onto the ground around the table, all tangled up in the gauze.

On the table there is also a metallic water pitcher, a makeup bag, a water glass, a bunch of grapes and a pen. Hidden in the folds of the gauze there is a spray can of insecticide bearing, as its label, a large skull and crossbones.

On the opposite side of the stage, there is a metal IV pole with an IV bag hanging from one of the pole's metal loops. The IV pole is clean and new. The bag is half-filled with colourless liquid.

In the shadows, stage left, there is an old upright piano and a synthesizer. Both are concealed under desiccated black fabric that looks like a cross between velvet and decaying rubber.

## Lights

Over the course of the performance, the lights change from a nice warm dappling of pinks and baby blues to a more and more warped state. Increasingly, the lights cool, and, increasingly, the stage is bathed in a tenebrous display of footlights and angled shafts of gothic hues.

Occasionally, under the brighter lights, the musician is dimly visible at the piano.

## Costume and Makeup

At the beginning of the show, Pochsy is swathed head to toe in gauze, almost like a mummy. For the rest of the show, she wears pink baby doll pyjamas, with matching pink lace-edged bloomers and lacy pink ankle socks. Her shoes are delicate white canvas sneakers. Her outfit is pristine.

Her face is chalk-white, except for the dark circles under her eyes, her thick black eyelashes and her blood-red lips. Later in the show, she will also have red cheeks. Her hair is black.

On her right wrist, there is a bandage of gauze and adhesive tape. Her head is bandaged in gauze.

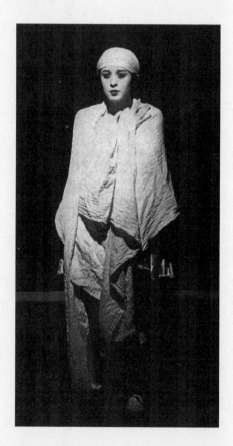

*(Pre-show music: Louis Armstrong's 'Saint James Infirmary.' As the song finishes, lights fade to black. Pin spot up on Pochsy, draped from head to toe in surgical gauze. There is a moment of silence, then she speaks with a terrible gravity, directly to the audience.)*

POCHSY: We live in a scary time. Advances we have made in science, medicine, and environmental awareness seem not to be keeping pace with the technological advances we have made. We are constantly bombarded by ominous information regarding ever-accelerating environmental poisoning, a continuing apocalyptic threat and mysterious and uncontrollable disease. All indicators point to the distinct possibility that we are a species bent on self-extinction. No one is safe. And there is no escape.

*(Music swells. Pochsy sings 'Everything's Falling Apart,' brightly, freely, winsomely.)*

Everything's falling apart,
But everyone's falling in love.

Seems like the end of the world is nigh,
But it's not over for you and I.
Oh, everything's falling apart,
But everyone's falling in love.

*(Lights up to full. Pochsy strips out of the gauze, revealing her pink baby doll pyjamas. She twirls around and dances with the IV pole. She rides it across the stage in a graceful arabesque.)*

What's that gloomy cloud above your head?
Fluffy toxic cloud of misery!
Take the psychic scissors,

Cut the rope of worry.
Watch that cloud fly away!

Oh, everything's falling apart,
But everyone's falling in love.

*(Pochsy twirls, untangles the IV tubing from the pole, presents it to the audience, as though in a magic show, then slips the IV needle beneath the bandage at her wrist and inserts it into her vein.)*

Ooh!

*(She swoons and dances.)*

Take my hand, fall into my eyes,
Walk along the beach with me,
Look up into the purple sky,
And at the shiny black ducks resting peacefully.
Oh! *(She steps lightly over an imagined duck.)*

Everything's falling apart,
But everyone's falling,
Filly-fally falling,

Everybody's falling,
Hear my love song calling yo-oo-o-o-oo-ou ...

*(Pochsy stops dancing, swoons again, and reclines on her bed. The music follows her, sensitively.)*

Everybody's falling in love.

*(As the song ends, she points her toes, pulls the IV pole closer to the bed, and strikes a pretty pose. Then she speaks.)*

When I think about Love, I think about all the sad and lonely people who wander through their whole lives without ever finding *(gravely)* that special someone. That person who will melt their heart and make them whole. That person who will be there for them. In the hard times.

*(Pause..)*

But then I think ... it's probably their own fault. They just don't have a positive attitude. And so they don't recognize Love when it comes knocking on their door. And they send Love right back out into the rain, where it slips on the top step of the fire escape and falls, and knocks its head on the railing. And then bounces off and knocks its head on the other railing. And then Love slides down, on its tailbone, till it lurches forward at the bottom, where Love cracks its skull. And lies there, paralyzed. Totally conscious and alert ... aware of everything ... seeing, and hearing, and feeling everything but ... unable to move.

*(She giggles.)*

I think I'm a little bit in love. With my doctor. Doctor Caligari.

*(She giggles again and squirms girlishly. Love music plays under.)*

I don't know; there's just something about him. Like the way that he looks at me. *(dreamy)* When he's examining me.
    It's like I'm the only one in the room.

*(She drapes herself alluringly across the bed. The IV tubing pulls taut.)*

I remember our first examination together: as I lay on his table, the thin cotton of my floral print dress draped damply over my youthful form, I stared into his eyes, and I knew that I wanted to be with him. *(rapturous)* Bound together with him in a madness of our own making. I wanted to take the disillusionment out of his eyes and fly away with him. Set up a practice in the slums of Calcutta.
    I think he likes me, too, 'cuz I don't know, but *(kittenish)* I don't think anybody could be sick enough to have as many tests done on them as I have had done on me.

*(Love music ends.)*

Love has made me the happiest girl in the world.

*(Pochsy picks up the telephone and begins to dial.)*

H-hello? Wh-I was just calling y- No! It didn't even RING! OH my GOD, that's SO WEIRD! HI-I-I! How ARE you? *(She listens, but possibly a little too briefly to hear.)* Oh, I'm pretty good. *(She listens, again very briefly.)* Oh, no, I don't think I want to go out with you anymore. Well, bec– I found somebody better than you. Yeah, he's a doctor. *(She smiles at the audience.)* Oh, no, I'm sorry… No, I don't want to be friends. No, I already have plenty of friends. *(She seems suddenly horrified.)* Oh, you can't live without me?

*(Pause.)*

Oh, well. 'Kay bye.

*(She hangs up. Sad music plays under. A cool pool of light appears at the foot of the bed, and Pochsy moves into it to pray. She moves the IV pole a little to one side, so the audience can see her better.)*

Dear Lord,
    Please forgive me for all of the evil and weak things I have done in my life. Please give me the courage and the strength to carry on. Open my lips, oh Lord, and I will sing Thy praises. I need a sign.

*(She sings 'I'll Believe.')*

> I'll believe in You,
> If You'll believe in me ...
> But not till then.
> If You're in the skies above me,
> Please, God, show me that You love me,
> I will obey You
> Then.

Please forgive me for all the people whom I have hurt, and grant them the strength and the clarity – and the wisdom – to forgive me too. And for those people who have hurt me, please, Lord ... *(She pauses. She looks intently at God.)* Find a way to hurt them back.

> If You'll just give a sign,
> Give me something that's all mine,
> Then I'll open up my heart,

I'll do my best,
I'll do my part ...

But not till then.

Love, Pochsy

*(Pochsy blows God a soft little kiss. Music ends. Lights return to 'normal' — as before, only cooler. For a moment, Pochsy just gazes at the audience.)*

You know, I think it's very important, even when you're not feeling well, to look your very best! You never know who might pop in and, well, *(intrigued)* it seems I'm going to be seeing a specialist!
    And besides,

*(She sings the 'Wonder Bra' jingle.)*

When you're looking good,
You feel good.
And when you feel good,
You look gre-e-eat!

And great is how I want to look, 'cuz *(intensely)* when I like what I see? I enjoy being me.

*(Pochsy reaches for her makeup case and pulls out a compact. She shows it to the audience and speaks as though in a TV commercial.)*

Starts off as a powder, but goes on so smooth and creamy ...

*(She applies red blush to her white cheeks.)*

It makes you seem lit from within.

*(She tilts her face up for the audience.)*

Is that about right?

*(Beat.)*

Oh, I know, what's right, right? I mean, it's so individual.

*(Pause.)*

You are what you believe yourself to be. Anything your mind can conceive and believe, it will achieve.

*(Pause.)*

Like, the other day, before I came here, I was going somewhere, and so I was on an escalator, but I was late to where I was going and so I was walking up the escalator. But up ahead of me on the escalator there was this couple, *(almost crying)* and they were standing side by side. So that I couldn't get by.

So I went up behind them and I said, *(waif-like)* 'Excuse me, please.' But they didn't listen. So I stood right up on my tiptoes and I went *(nasty, heavy sigh)* 'H-H-H-H-H-H-H!'

*(She is suddenly very placid.)*

Not only did they step aside but I could tell from the looks on their faces that they felt like shit.

You see, it's astonishing how very short a time it takes for very wonderful things to happen.

Believing is magic.

*(The lights dim and cool a little more. Pochsy notices. She drapes herself in a different direction across the bed. She rolls the IV pole to the other side of the bed, pulling it by its tubing.)*

Before I came here, I had a job. I worked at Mercury Packers. Where I packed mercury. And when I first got here, the nurse – the one with the fat ass – she asked me a whole bunch of questions that she had to get answers to to put down on this form that she was filling in. So, she asked me, when I worked at Mercury Packers, did I ever handle the mercury with my hands? So I said, *(as if to a child)* 'Well, if I had gloves on, then I wouldn't, but if I didn't ... then I would.' *(She rolls her eyes.)*

And besides, if you spill the mercury and it falls on the floor and bursts into all those shiny, sparkly little bubbles? The best way to pick it up is to go like *(she licks her finger and mimes picking up a mercury ball with it)* ... that.

I think that nurse is just jealous of me. Because she knows Doctor Caligari likes me.

*(Pochsy picks up a get-well card from her table and reads.)*

'Pillows,
Fluffy clouds,
Cotton candy,
Towels just out of the dryer.'

*(She shows the front of the card to the audience.)*

It says that!

*(She opens the card and reads.)* 'Thought you could use some soft, comforting words.' *(to the audience)* And I can.

*(She reads.)* 'Dear Pochsy, So sorry to hear that you might be dying.' *(to the audience)* Aww.

'We just wanted to write and let you know that you are probably the most wonderful person that we have ever, ever met.' *(to the audience)* Wow.

*(She reads.)* 'We miss your precious, smiling face and the splendid tinkling of your laughter.'

*(Pochsy squeals.)*

'And we hope that, as you wither away into a little wisp of a thing, and that even if you do die young, you can rest in the knowledge that your flashy smile has been seared into the hearts of all of those whose lives you have touched with your glowing, pink little fingers.'

*(She picks up a pen and writes.)* 'Love, from all your friends at Mercury Packers.'

34

*(Pause. She reads what she has written.)*

*(Icily)* Wow. That's *so* nice.

*(Pochsy places the card and pen on the table. Lights cool. She sings 'Squid Song' a cappella.)*

> There's a star falling down in the sky,
> There's a full moon shining on me,
> But I feel so sad and lonesome,
> There's a squid where my heart used to be.

I keep trying to tell them, but they don't believe me. But you see, because it is a squid – and conscious – it is able, when it wants to, to pull up its tentacles and to form itself into the shape of a heart. *(She traces a finger around her heart.)* Which is why it doesn't show up on the X-rays.

And because it is a squid – and conscious – it is able to pump my blood. Which is why it doesn't show up on the monitors.

But because it is a squid, it then pumps algae through my veins. *(She traces a finger along a vein.)* Which is why *(like a baby)* I'm not feeling well.

*(She squirms and fusses with her baby dolls, causing them to drape more alluringly from her form.)*

Even Doctor Caligari doesn't believe me.

*(Pause.)*

That will be his downfall.

*(She reclines, invitingly.)*

Sometimes, when I'm lying in my bed, I can feel it moving. *(Her fingers trace the tendons of her throat.)* Sometimes, late at night, I can feel one of its tentacles creeping up my throa– *(she gags).*
And I have to swallow to keep it down.

*(She does.)*

But I don't know how much longer I can keep on swallowing. And I'm a little bit afraid that one of these nights, when I'm dreaming, *(she whispers)* the squid will make its way up to my brain.
And right about now, I can't afford to lose control.
I have something important on my mind.

*(A country music intro plays under. Moonlight lighting.)*

When I think about it sometimes, when I think about the squid in my chest, I get feeling kinda lonesome and ... blue. But I know, deep inside I know that out there, somewhere, there's someone who's gonna know, just by looking into my eyes, that there is a squid in my chest. And I know that he will know just what to do.

*(Pochsy sings 'Squid Song.')*

> In a cold and lonesome Nebraska town,
> There's a doctor waitin' for me,
> And the look in my eyes will soften his heart,
> As he touches the squid in me.

We will meet in the local Nebraska-town bar. I will pull up in my white Chevy truck, and I will get out of it with my knees together. *(Pochsy gets out of bed.)* As I stand, I will feel one squid tentacle thrust itself deep into my thigh, as another reaches up and tickles at the tip of my uvula. *(She gags.)* I will feel myself passing out, but I will be bathed in the neon light from the Budweiser sign up ahead *(she is bathed in pink light)*, and as I stumble through the doorway to the bar, I will be backlit by the huge Texaco sign in behind *(she is backlit in red)*, and my youthful form, too young to die, will be visible through the thin cotton of my floral-print dress.

*(Pochsy stares at the IV pole for a moment, as though she is seeing it for the first time.)*

I will ask the bartender – a tall, scrawny man *(she looks up at the IV pole's metal loops)* wearing silver spectacles – I will ask him for a beer. No glass. And I will hear, from off-screen, a voice say, 'That's okay, Jim. That beer's on me.'

The shot will widen to reveal a tall, lanky man *(she rolls the IV pole over to her other side)* with hollow, sad eyes *(she glances again at the metal loops)* set far apart. He will be wearing faded Levi's jeans that are torn so naturally at the knee, and a white cotton T-shirt that is frayed so naturally at the neck. And I can tell, from the look in his eyes, and from the white doctor's coat on the stool beside him, that he is the one.

*(Pochsy stares deep into the IV pole's 'eyes' and moves slowly toward it.)*

There's a cold, hard wind blowing all around,
There's a vortex sucking from the west,
But a sad lonely man's staring deep in my eyes,
Soothing the squid in my chest.

We will rise and glide wordlessly onto the dance floor *(she twirls with the IV pole)*, where he will place a cool hand on my hot back. We will sway slowly and, as we do, I will turn slowly from pink, to white, to baby blue. *(She presses her cheek up against the pole.)* And as I gag gently onto the white cotton of his T-shirt, the tip of a tentacle will poke from my mouth.

*(She leans against the IV pole for support.)*

There's a gust of wind rolling down a hill,
There's a bright orange cloud in the sky,
But a sad lonely man's rocking me in his arms,
Rocking the squid and I.

He will lift me up and carry me out to the parking lot *(she glides to the bed and lies down on it)*, where he will lay me down on the cool asphalt. The tiny beads of perspiration on my hairless upper lip will be multicoloured, lit up by the Budweiser sign on the one side and by the Texaco sign on the other. And as my body becomes wracked by convulsions *(she actually gags)*, he will pull, from his faded hip pocket, a stethoscope. *(She writhes, sensually.)* Oh.

There's a herd of clouds rushing overhead,
There's a stinging rain pouring down,
But a sad lonely man's touched the hot, squirming squid,
And blackbirds fly all around.

Back at his place, back at his farm *(she sits up and perches on the edge of the bed)*, we will sit on the old porch swing and swing back and forth, as he tells me the sad story of his pretty wife who died a few years back. Mysteriously. Right after they insulated their house.

The tears will pour from his eyes and onto the porch floor and I will tear the kerchief from my long curly hair and hand it to him to wipe up those tears. But the pain will be too much for me to bear and I will be forced to stand out at the edge of the porch and stare out over the failing crops.

*(She walks down to the front edge of the stage.)*

A gust of wind will come up from behind and toss my long curly hair across my face. I will try to brush it away, but I won't be able to get it all. *(ultra-waify)* There'll be a little wisp left.

*(She pulls on the IV tubing and rolls the IV pole up behind her.)*

But the small Nebraska-town doctor will come up behind me and place an arm around me, from behind *(she wraps her own arm around herself)*, so that his forearm spreads and looks bigger than it actually is. He will turn my face toward him *(she turns her own face toward 'him')* and brush that wisp away.

*(She stares into the IV pole's 'eyes.')*

And as our lips draw near, the shirt will fall from his hairless back. And as our lips part, the floral print dress will fall from my back. *(adorably)* Which is also hairless.

*(She reaches up and tenderly touches the IV bag.)*

And when our lips meet … when we kiss … the squid will be washed away.

*(Pochsy waltzes with the IV pole. She caresses the IV bag, wraps her arm around the pole and rides away on it like a ballerina. She glides once around the stage, then collides with the bed, stumbles and falls gracefully over the foot of bed. Music ends. Lights return to 'normal': cooler, with footlights now creeping in.)*

Mmmm … Water.

*(Pochsy reaches for her water pitcher and glass.)*

Every cell in your body needs it. And it helps contribute to a healthy, glowing complexion.

*(She pours a glass of dark, murky water.)*

I drink at least eight to ten glasses a day.

*(She drinks it.)*

You know, *(she picks up a bunch of grapes)* I have come to that point in my life where I have to start thinking about whether or not I should have a baby. I've made up a list of pros and cons *(she sprays grapes with insecticide)*, but it just seems to confuse me more than anything else.

Oh! *(reassuringly, referring to spray can)* Just in case bugs.

*(She eats a grape.)*

All I know is that I want a family that's a team. A family like my own happy family. *(She eats another grape.)* With a happy mother, and a happy father, a happy brother … and a happy, happy sister.

*(Pochsy picks up telephone and begins to dial.)*

H-Hello? Oh my– No, I was just ca– NO, it didn't even RING! Oh my GOD, that's so WEIRD! HI-I-I-I, how ARE yo-o-o-ou? *(She listens, again a little too briefly to hear much.)* Oh, I'm pretty good – Oh wow, that's wonderful! Mom and Dad must be so proud of you! … No, no, I'm really happy that you're very fulfilled in your career and that you're getting married to a really great guy – Oh, but listen. *(She glances at the audience.)* There's something I meant to mention last time we talked, but I forgot, so I thought I would bring it up now. *(Beat.)* You were adopted. *(Beat.)* I just thought you should kno– *(too cheerily)* Okay, I'll talk to you soon – 'kay bye.

*(She hangs up hard. She stares at the phone. She stares at the audience.)*

*(Chillingly)* Well, she was.

*(Pochsy hurls her grapes across the stage. They scatter. She stares at the audience again. She points her toes.)*

*(Sweetly)* Oopsydaisy.

*(Pause.)*

Um … A few months ago, I was invited up to a friend's chalet, deep in the rocky, spiky, northern wilderness. After a couple of days, I could feel all the yucky city stuff just kind of dripping off of me, and I felt myself becoming more at peace, not only with

my surroundings, but with myself as well. On the third after-
noon, I found myself staring out a window into the icy, spiky,
snowy wilderness, and my friend came and stood beside me for
a moment. And we shared a moment. Then my friend asked me
if I would help her with the lunch dishes. So I told her to fuck
right off, and I went out on the snowmobile. After about five
miles the snowmobile ran out of gas. And so I left it there to rust.

*(With some difficulty, she climbs up onto the headboard, where she*
*perches prettily, though precariously, for the rest of the story.)*

I found myself standing at the rocky, spiky edge of a lake that was
completely covered over in ice. Out in the middle of the lake
there was a little island, and about a hundred yards to the
south of the island there was a little herd of deer – or a little
grouping – *(she searches for the correct term)* a *cluster* of deer.

One of the deer had separated himself from the group and
was making his way very slowly, and tentatively, towards the
little island. As I watched him, I realized that he was testing the
ice ... making sure that it was safe for all the other little deer to
follow. I held my breath so that he would not go crashing through
the ice, and I prayed for him to make it across safely.

*(She smiles, pleased with herself.)* Which he did.

Then, one by one, all the other little deer made their way very slowly and tentatively towards the little island, and I held my breath and prayed for each and every one of them to make it across safely.

*(Thrilled with herself)* Which they did.

Once all the little deer had made it safely onto the little island, I watched them as they disappeared into the little woods of the little island, nibbling on little icicles as they went.

But I found myself spiralling down into an unspeakable despair, as I realized that in five years those deer would no longer be there. They would be forced to move further north when the new highway came through, or else they would wind up slaughtered on the side of the road.

I was just about to bash my head out on the rocks, when I heard from behind me a little rustling. I turned around to see what it was, and there, standing all by himself at the edge of the woods was a little deer. He was a solo deer. And it was as if he had come to tell me, 'It's okay, Pochsy, everything's going to be okay.' It was like we were having a little conversation.

And as we conversed, as it were, I felt something slide into my left hand. I looked down to see what it was, and there in my hand was another hand. Darker than my own.

I followed the hand along to the arm, up to the shoulder, to the head, and realized that I was holding the hand of a Native Canadian Indian! And it was as if he had come to tell me, 'It's okay, Pochsy! Everything's going to be okay.'

Then the little deer came over and sat down beside us, and I held out my hand to him, and he placed his little deer paw in my hand … *(she searches for the correct word)* his … hoof … and the three of us just kind of sat there, making a sort of psychic-spiritual triangle. Did you know that the triangle is the strongest geometric form there is? I had never felt so connected to the earth as a whole in my whole life! And I really did feel that everything was going to be okay.

*(Pause.)*

But then something occurred to me. I realized that something was a little bit funny. The deer should not have come so close. He should not be so bold.

I looked over at him, and he looked back at me with his big deer eyes … But there, in the corner of his mouth, was a little bit of foam.

So I looked over at the Indian, 'cuz I thought he might know what to do, because he was an Indian … But there, in the corner of his mouth, was a little bit of foam.

So then the deer took off back into the woods, and, as he did, I felt the Indian's hand slip out of mine and he took off into the woods as well. So then I was alone. *(Pause.)* And feeling a little bit blue.

*(Pause.)*

But at least for that one moment, I really did feel that everything was going to be okay.

*(Pochsy smiles serenely. Then she wipes a little bit of foam from the corner of her mouth. She swoons. She slips from the headboard and tentatively creeps down to the foot of the bed to pray.)*

Dear Lord,

Pursuant to my last prayer, I find myself, at this time, in need of a stronger commitment from You, and·I'm wondering if it isn't perhaps time You took a good hard look at Yourself.

The test results are still inconclusive; it seems the specialist was also foiled by the squid.

*(Glacial)* That will be his downfall.

I understand that You're very busy at this time, but it isn't as if I don't have important things on my mind, too.

Success is an attitude, Lord.

Get Yours right.

Love, Pochsy.

*(She blows God a kiss. Lights grow colder still.)*

When I grow sick of the small Nebraska-town doctor – as I will – when it becomes apparent that he never actually washed away the squid – he simply anaesthetized it temporarily – I will pack all my floral print dresses into my soft-sided luggage, and I will wheel them out into the hallway.

*(Pochsy wheels the IV pole to centre stage.)*

The small Nebraska-town doctor will try to stop me, and I will want to say *(softly, to the IV pole)*, 'Oh, baby.' But there will be a rising in my throat as a tentacle reaches out and slaps him across the face. *(She drops back onto the bed.)*

I will feel myself passing out, but I will be bathed in the orange light that pours through the window from the Stelco sign high above. *(She is bathed in orange light.)* And I will hear a voice, calling ...

*(Music under. Pochsy sings 'Dark Green Isle.')*

> Far away on a dark green isle,
> There's a place you can rest awhile,
> There's nothing to bring,
> You don't need a thing,
> Except something important on your mind.

*(She rises from the bed.)*

I will make my way down to the small Nebraska-town docks, where I will find and steal a small outboard motor boat that will take me down the Nebraska-town river and out to the sea.

*(She crosses again, with the IV pole, to centre.)*

When I reach the calm, clear centre of the ocean, the squid will be pacified temporarily as it senses the proximity of other sea creatures. My IV unit – which I will have brought with me up till now simply as ballast – will be rendered redundant at this point by the increasing weight of the important thing on my mind, and I will cast it into the ocean.

46

*(Pochsy extracts the IV needle from her wrist, winces, and pushes the IV pole away. It rolls off into the shadows at the side of the stage.)*

> My spirit soars free,
> As I trail behind me,
> Petroleum rainbows in the sea.

*(Pochsy weakens and leans on the footboard. She collapses in convulsions onto the bed. Drumbeats pound. Pochsy grips the bed posts hard and breathes very deeply. Lights turn icy – it's almost all footlights now, and her shadow grows huge against the back of the stage. She tosses her head back and snaps to.)*

Three days later, I wake up on the beach. I've been asleep for days, but my legs are smooth and my breath is minty fresh, so I know I've come to the right place. My boat has lodged itself on the rocky, spiky shore of the dark green island, and I get out of it with my knees together.

*(She rises from the bed.)*

As I stand, I feel one squid tentacle thrust itself deep into my thigh, as another reaches up, wraps around my skull and begins to tickle at the soft front part of my brain.

*(She drapes herself against the headboard.)*

I feel myself passing out – but I am bathed in the purple light that bounces off the flesh of a whale who is resting peacefully on the rocks. A gust of wind comes up and blows my savage, curly hair across my face. I try to brush it away, but I can't get it all. *(feigning distress)* There's a little wisp left.

So I look around for someone to brush it away for me.

*(Pochsy walks toward the edge of the stage.)*

In the distance, standing at the edge of the water, I see a small, blonde, brown little girl. She is feeding Minute Rice to a three-legged bird. The child moves toward me and, as she does, the bird gallops along behind her and tugs at her bathing-suit bottom, exposing a tender white strip of flesh that has not yet been kissed by the sun. *(Pochsy mimics the Coppertone ad.)* I follow the child inland. I don't know why. It just *feels* right.

The child leads me into the dark green forest of the dark green island. In the forest is a clearing. In the clearing stands a boxer. I climb into the ring. *(She climbs over the footboard, onto the bed.)* I don't know why. It just *feels* right.

*(She stares at something invisible. Her jaw drops.)*

And I realize that I am standing in a boxing ring with Mickey Rourke! He is leaning up against the ropes so that his arms spread and look bigger than they actually are, and his knees are spread engagingly apart. We chat for a while just about … stuff. And I can tell, from the look in his eyes, and from the IRA tattoo on his arm, that he's got something really important on his mind. And I want to ask him, 'Hey, Mickey, what is that important thing on your mind?' because I'm hoping that it's the same important thing that's on my mind but *(she gags)* squid's got my tongue *(she convulses)* and I am falling.

*(She slides down the footboard and grips the slats of the bed.)*

I'm on the hood of a car. A car filled with happy, laughing teenagers wearing bustiers. They are drinking brightly coloured soft drinks, and I can hear them chanting, through the foam in their mouths, 'Pochsy, just do it. Just do it.' And so I stand up on the hood of the car. But they continue to chant, 'Pochsy, JUST DO IT.' And so I say, 'Do WHAT?' But the car swerves *(she convulses)*, and I'm on the side of the road.

*(She stares out into the audience. Drums beat louder.)*

I'm at a fork in the road. And I realize that I don't want fifteen minutes of fame; I want a career. I need a family that's a team!
So I take the road less travelled.

*(She stands up on the bed, holds her hand over her eyes and looks out.)*

There are thousands of people on the road less travelled.
People who create their own reality. People who play hard. And I can tell, from the looks in their eyes, that they all have something important on their minds, and so I know I'm going the right way.

*(She walks across the front edge of the bed, which bends and creaks frighteningly with her steps.)*

In the distance, I see a shiny, sparkly thing. *(A shaft of light hits the IV pole.)*
I want it.
But it's hard to see 'cuz of all the people on the road less travelled: wet women, wrapped in towels, shaking droplets of water from their tangle-free curls; finely muscled men wearing nothing but jeans … and babies.

*(Pochsy struggles up the slope of the bed, in the direction of the IV pole.)*

The shiny, sparkly thing is moving up the hill. And I know you don't get anything unless you go out on a limb, *(she recoils from something in the air before her)* but a throng of refugees comes pouring over the hill, screaming and tearing at their own faces. When they reach me they stop. *(Drums out.)* And dance as if their lives depended on it!

*(Drums in. Pochsy dances madly.)*

I call out to them, 'Dream great dreams and make them come true! Set a goal! Make a plan! WRITE IT DOWN!'

*(She falls and crawls.)*

The shiny, sparkly thing is moving over the hill. But I know that anything my mind can conceive, and believe, it will achieve.

*(She stares at the IV pole. With great effort, she drags herself up onto the headboard. She wraps her legs around the headboard and perches, very precariously. Leaning out, she prays.)*

Dear Lord,

I regret to inform You that Your services will no longer be required. Your position has been rendered redundant. Best of luck in Your future endeavours.

Love, Pochsy.

*(She blows God a cold little kiss. She looks at the IV pole. Drumbeats stop. She sees something beyond the IV pole. Dangerously, she leans out farther.)*

Stretched out over the hill, in a perfect line, are one thousand women wearing floral print dresses. And standing with them, in a perfect line, are one thousand men wearing faded Levi's jeans that are torn so naturally at the knee and white cotton T-shirts that are frayed so naturally at the neck.

As the men turn the women's faces toward them, a stinging rain comes pouring down and bursts on the hard ground into shiny, sparkly little bubbles. And as their two thousand pairs of lips draw near, there is a rising in their throats.

*(There is a rising in Pochsy's throat.)*

And as their lips part *(she convulses)*, two thousand tentacles poke from their mouths *(she convulses again)*, and tug.

*(She has a very powerful convulsion.)*

And two thousand squids pour onto the ground.

*(She collapses, her legs still wrapped around the headboard. There is a long silence as she realizes she is in an ugly pose. She smiles for the audience, points her toes, then speaks with difficulty.)*

I will always believe in the ideal. And I will not look back with regret. Because I hope to be remembered, not recalled.

I am, after all, me.

*(She gauges her position, then, after a moment, struggles slowly and inelegantly back into bed. She arranges her legs, places her hands in*

*ballet position, and points her toes. Sad music plays. She sings 'I'm Too Young to Die.')*

> I'm too young to die,
> I'm just a little cutie-pie,
> But though the boys are calling, calling,
> I believe the sky is falling,
> I'm too young to die.

*(She convulses and dances in bed. Bubbles float up from behind her.)*

> I'm too young to die,
> A floofy fluffy sweetie-pie,
> But though the light is bright above me,
> I'm so sad to leave this lovely
> House of cards.

*(A mirror ball lights up and turns, and sparkles flood the stage.)*

> I'm too young to die,
> My little life's gone flashing by,
> But though the foam creeps up the beach,
> My own marine life's out of reach,
> And warm and safe inside.

*(She perches, trembling, on the edge of her bed.)*

We live at a time when imagining a meaningful future is irrational and unrealistic.

*(Big smile.)*

The choice of a new generation!

*(Exuberantly, she throws her fist into the air, as she might in a Pepsi commercial. Then she wilts down onto the bed. She gazes at the audience.)*

I hope that you're all falling in love.

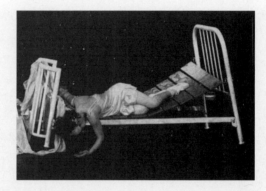

*(Pochsy blows the audience a kiss and daintily wipes the foam from her mouth. She arranges her baby dolls around her, then collapses, draped artfully over the edge of the bed. All lights fade to black except the mirror ball, which fades to black more slowly.)*

**The End**

# Oh, baby
## (Pochsy's Adventures by the Sea)

## Performance History

*Oh, baby (Pochsy's Adventures by the Sea)* was first presented at the Fringe of Toronto festival in July 1993. It then toured to festivals in Sudbury and Edmonton and to Women in View in Vancouver. A full production was presented by Pochsy Productions at Factory Theatre's Studio Theatre in Toronto in November 1993.

Pochsy: Karen Hines
The Musician: Greg Morrison

Text, lyrics and melodies by Karen Hines
Directed by and written in collaboration with Sandra Balcovske
Music and sound by Greg Morrison
Set and lighting by Michel Charbonneau
Costume by Wendy White
Original shell design by Campbell Manning
Slag generously provided by CP Rail

## Set

The set is a gargantuan aqua-blue clam shell – a half-shell – about eight feet deep, six feet wide and four feet high. It sits, convex side up, on a slate-grey pile of slag fourteen feet wide by fourteen feet deep. The slag is surrounded by a moat of water.

A single acid-yellow daisy is growing in the slag by the edge of the water.

The clam shell is too steep on its sides to be comfortably walked on, but its front slope is not: its wide peaks and valleys can accommodate lounging, perching, walking and even dancing. A white rotary dial telephone is perched precariously on one sloping side of the shell. At the front lip of the shell, there is a bottle of sunscreen, a brightly coloured brochure and a brightly coloured bon voyage card.

There is a picnic basket sitting on the slag at stage right. It is covered with a little gauze. The contents, which will not be seen until late in the show, include a bottle of clear fizzy liquid that glows in the dark, a realistic yet disturbingly rubbery fish and a huge glass bowl of maraschino cherries.

There is a pen hidden in a crack in the seashell.

The musician is not visible: his synthesizer is perched high up, behind the audience.

## Costume

Pochsy wears a creamy, gauzy little tunic, with cream-coloured streamlined pantaloons: the effect is reminiscent of a bathing costume from the thirties. She wears delicate white canvas sneakers on her feet. Her head is wrapped in a matching scarf, though upon closer inspection, it is clearly a medical bandage.

**Makeup**

Her face is white. Her hair is black. Her eyes are thick-lashed and kohl-smudged. There are very dark circles under her eyes. Her lips are blood red.

*(As the audience enters, there is a sound recording of nature. As curtain time draws near, the sounds become more defined and more disturbing: jungle birds seem to mingle with Arctic foxes, waves crash and mountain goats shriek. As the house lights fade, the sounds crescendo, animals scream, then all is black and silent. Spotlight up on Pochsy, on her back, draped across the half-shell.)*

POCHSY: Ooooh!

*(She sits up, with difficulty, arranges her bathing costume around her, then points her toes.)*

Sometimes, I find myself feeling a little bit overwhelmed by all the suffering and despair in the world around me. Sometimes, it's all just a little too much for my little soul to bear. So I say, when the going gets tough … escape.

*(Music in.)*

Take off.

*(She spins on the shell.)*

And take yourself on a Dream Vacation.

*(Lights surge up. Pochsy sings 'Funny Little World.')*

> Every day's a holiday when dreams come true,
> I'm longing for a sunny day or two or three.
> The tears in your eyes aren't here to stay,
> The sun shines brighter every day …

*(She reaches her arms up into the bright hot light, then recoils in pain. Music suddenly out.)*

Ouch!

*(There is a silence. Then she grins at the audience. Music back in.)*

It's a funny little world!

*(She catches a green and blue beach ball that is thrown to her from somewhere high above. The ball looks like the world. She dances with it for a moment. Then she speaks over the continuing melody.)*

The truth is, I had to get away. I was feeling a little bit under the weather, and fading away into a little wisp of a thing. *(She sways.)* I'm feeling much better now, though. Seems I didn't need professional help. Just a bit of sunshine and a splash in the water to put the roses back in my cheeks. *(She pinches her pale white cheeks.)* And now ...

*(She reclines alluringly.)*

I'm just languishing!

*(Over the following verse, she rolls the ball along one leg, like in a thirties postcard.)*

> Merrily towards the waterfall we float along,
> Nibbling fancy sandwiches, we sing a song.
> We've miles and miles and miles to go,
> Miles and miles to row row row.

*(She almost drops the ball, then scoops it up to her chest.)*

Life is but a dream come true!

*(She perches on the front lip of the shell.)*

Make a wish upon the evening star,
Bathe me in the afterglow.
Watch the star fall into the sea,
Frolic in the undertow.
Oh, no.

Though one less star is shining,
Every ocean has a silver lining.
Boop boop bee doo!

*(She dances more exuberantly with the ball.)*

Little bit of paradise, huh? Open skies, and a beach to die for!

*(She jumps off the shell and onto the slag, which crunches loudly and is clearly very painful to walk on. She sits down on the shell and tucks her feet up.)*

I wanna lie out in the sun all day long. It warms me straight through to the heart. But I know no tan is a safe tan, so …

*(She grabs her sunscreen and squirts some high into the air. She tosses the bottle to the ground, catches the cream in both hands, then rubs it on to her arms.)*

Makes my skin feel soft and smooth. Makes it look like fresh young skin. All over.

*(She traces her fingers over the bandages on her head.)*

Giving me total peace of mind.

*(She sings.)*

>    Don't you bother worrying what tomorrow holds,
>    Life is a happy accident and off we go.
>    The future is looking bright and rosy,
>    We've got two birds in the bush
>    And a pocket full of po-oh-oh-sies ...

*(She swoons.)*

>    Life on earth is heaven,
>    I can hear the angels sing ...

*(She listens. There is silence.)*

>    It's a funny little world.

Ha ha ha ha ha ha ha.

*(As the song finishes, Pochsy tosses the beach ball out into audience and prances around on the shell for a moment. Then she perches on top of the seashell, points her toes and speaks.)*

Since I've been here, I've been spending a lot of time alone with my thoughts, and getting back in touch with my, um *(she searches for the word)* ... self.

All cozied up in the arms of Mother Earth and Father Sky.

And I've been reflecting on my relationship with God, which is kind of interesting; it's not really an interactive relationship — mostly, I talk and he ... listens.

Which is good for me, because then I have to figure things out for myself. Listen to my own inner voice. Which guides me in the direction *I* want to go.

*(She twists a dangling head bandage around her finger.)*

The plane ride over was a trip in itself! The food looked great – there was a choice of steak or, um, beef – but I was feeling a little bit delicate, so I just sat back and watched the movie. It was a double bill of *Testament* and *The Day After*.

And I laughed my head off!

But then the little girl in the seat behind me started to kick the back of my chair. I asked her to stop, but she seemed, somehow, unable to. So I turned around and asked her mother *(graciously)* what kind of a mother she was.

She didn't seem to know.

So when the little girl got up to go to the bathroom, I waited for a minute, and then I followed her. I went to where she was standing in line, in her little sundress, with her little pig legs sticking out the bottom … and I kicked her in the back.

I explained everything to her. How irritating it was.

*(Pause.)*

Well, I'm nothing if I'm not honest.

*(She strikes a new pose.)*

When I got to my hotel room, there was an invitation on my pillow to the manager's cocktail party. So I slipped into something a little more whimsical and went down to the waterfront.

There were other people there too. But I had a good time anyway!

*(A lovely, if slightly unsettling, melody wafts under.)*

The water was perfectly calm. Except for the sea foam, which sparkled in the twilight. Far away, loons were crying. And all the tables were decorated with vases filled with fresh-cut trilliums.

*(She thinks.)* Trillia.

*(She drapes herself sideways across the shell.)*

I draped myself down the length of a lounge chair and accepted my complimentary cocktail and little bits of pheasant marinated in Memories of Tibet.

   Then the manager himself came over and sat down on the edge of my chaise. I introduced myself, but he just stared out over the water and watched the foam creep up the beach. He said if I had any suggestions to make during the week to *please* let him know. So I suggested that he drop about forty pounds, and that he might think about chopping down the maple grove to put in a tennis court. I don't play, myself, but *(sibylline)* I do like to watch.

Then he handed me this.

*(She reads from the brochure.)*

'Welcome. To the Last Resort.

'Whether you're heavy-hearted or light-headed, the Last Resort offers sanctuary for those too fragile for this world.'

*(She laughs with fragility.)*

'Rest peacefully in the privacy of your fully appointed suite. Then enjoy all the natural wonders that await you. Come… *(she steps tentatively onto the slag)* walk beside still waters. Lie down in green pastures. Our staff, they'll comfort you. And prepare a table before you. Beneath the starry skies of the Love Lounge, your cup runneth over.'

*(She crumples the brochure and tosses it onto the ground.)*

'Group rates available.'

*(She smacks a mosquito and glares at God. She falls to her knees, causing the slag to make a disturbing crunching sound.)*

Ouch.

Dear Lord,

Sorry I haven't contacted You for a while, but … *(she thinks)* I haven't needed anything lately.

As You may or may not know, I am vacationing now on a little island just off the coast of the state of Grace. The weather is unusually perfect, but the mosquitoes are bad. *(She flutters her lashes.)* Just thought You should know. *(She scratches the bite.)* Wish You were here.

Love, Pochsy.

*(She blows God a kiss.)*

My first morning here, I was still feeling a little bit fragile, so I treated myself to breakfast in bed and chatted with my chambermaid, Hazel, because I think it's important to listen to what people have to say – even the dull and the ignorant.

She told me about her babies, and how she has to have another job to support them. I asked her what she does. Apparently, she sells seashells … by the … um …

*(Slightly fuddled, she tucks a dangling bit of bandage behind her ear.)*

As we chatted, I noticed that she was using an abrasive cleanser. On my vanity. *(dripping condescension)* I said, 'Hazel. That's not a green product.' *(then, cavalier)* And I took it out of her hands and I poured it down the sink! Then I put on something light and frothy and went out for a ride in a glass-bottomed boat.

Through the glass on the bottom of the boat, I could see little muskies and trout swimming by, with bubbles pouring out of their mouths. As though they were calling to me. I dangled my fingers in the water, which made them feel soft and supple, with *(she sniffs them)* just a hint of pine. I asked the driver boy about the big turtles, which I had seen advertised in the brochure. He said he hadn't seen any for months. *(frosty)* So I made him give me my money back.

*(Pause.)*

Do you ever get the feeling, when you're in a little boat, on the water, that there's something scary down there?

*(She laughs nervously and tucks all her limbs in tight.)*

Um ... I have to call a friend.

*(She picks up the phone.)*

Yes, I'd like to make a call and charge it to my room, please? *(She listens.)* Room 222. *(She listens.)* Oh, um ... 1 ... 976 ... C-H-A-T.

*(Phone chat music plays under. It is, at once, cheesy and dreamy. Pochsy speaks wispily, as though she is in a phone chat ad.)*

Hi. My name's Pochsy. I'm five feet tall, I have curly hair, and I weigh about a hundred pounds. I was just wondering if anyone out there wants to chat with me.

*(She waits. And waits. And waits. Then she starts, delighted.)*

Hello? *(She listens.)* Yes it is. What's your name? ... Oh, hello, 'Tom.' Would you like to have an 'intimate conversation?' ... Oh, good, me neither! What do you look like?... Oh. Ha ha. That's funny! ... Oh, nothing, it's just that *(she glances incredulously at the audience)* I'm really healthy and attractive too!

What do I 'like'? Well, *(puzzled)* um, the smell of burning wood makes me wistful ... ?

Why? What do you 'like'?

*(She listens, disturbed by what 'Tom' 'likes.')*

Oh.

Listen, Tom, I think I have another call coming in, could you hold on for a sec–?

*(She depresses the receiver button, slowly slides the receiver onto its cradle, then looks down at the phone and feigns surprise.)*

Oopsydaisy.

*(Pause.)*

Do you ever get that feeling, even when you're on vacation, that you would like to go away?

*(Pochsy drifts down the shell. Warily, she makes her way onto the slag. Cautiously, she steps to the water's edge. She catches sight of herself reflected in the water. Love music plays. She sings 'Someone Good Enough For Me.')*

> I long to take
> A seaside holiday escape
> And shed this dread ennui.
> I long to be
> With someone good enough for me.

*(She picks the little daisy that is growing in the slag and daintily plucks the petals, one by one.)*

> I would take the chance,
> A seaside holiday romance
> Would be so heavenly.
> With just one kiss
> He'd take me away from all of this.

*(She leans against one side of the shell, her forearm draped across her
forehead à la Camille.)*

>     And if I grew lovesick,
>     He would bathe my fevered face,
>     Hold me in his strong embrace,
>     Heal me with his fingertips,
>     Catch the pearls as they fall from my lips.

>     I would live to see
>     Eternity
>     With someone good enough

>     For me.

*(She sniffs the mangled little flower, then sees it, is horrified by it, and
flings it away. As the song ends, she swoons and drapes herself across
the shell. She just watches the audience for a moment.)*

The other day I was on the beach, just sort of ... hanging around
near the lifeguard.

   He dropped his sunglasses in the sand and so I leaned over
*(she demonstrates, fetchingly)* to pick them up for him. He said it
was very attractive, the way that I did that. I said, 'Oh really? I
wasn't even conscious of it.'

*(She inches down toward the water.)*

I asked him if he would like to go for a dip with me. He said he
wasn't much of a swimmer, but that he would watch. And then
he warned me about the undertow.

*(She stops. She looks into the water.)*

Lifeguards are such alarmists.

*(There is a very long pause.)*

*(Quietly)* At home, I have a job. I work at Mercury Packers. Where I pack mercury.

My last day before I left was the company physical, and when I got there, there was a long lineup, but everyone let me go ahead of them so that I wouldn't have to wait in line.

In the examination room, I lay down on the table wearing an examination gown so ethereal a harsh word would send it flying away. The nurse took my blood, and the doctor asked me a series of questions, one of which was, did I plan on having any children. He stared at me intently, and so I stared right back at him, and said, 'Why? *(She winks.)* You offering?'

I could tell by the looks on their faces that something was fishy.

Sure enough, when I left the examination, everyone was applauding for me. They had announced Employee of the Month. Guess who?

*(As though deeply moved)* I made a speech to them, through the tears in my eyes. I thanked them for deeming me better than everybody. *(Beat.)* I used sincerity. And the tears rolled down my cheeks and onto the floor, where they burst apart into a thousand sparkling bubbles. Then all my friends waved goodbye, and ... somebody handed me a cheque.

*(She picks up the bon voyage card and reads.)*

'To help make your trip an enjoyable one,
Go light on the luggage but not on the fun!'

*(She laughs half-heartedly.)*

'Dear Pochsy,

Just wanted to write and wish you a 'bon voyage.' Words can't begin to express how much we miss you already. Some of us are even hurling ourselves at walls, we're so distraught. We want you to know how much we appreciate the sacrifices you have made, and your lifelong dedication.

Wishing you nothing ... but the best,
The Management,
Mercury Packers
(A subsidiary of Lead World.)

*(She sniffs the card.)*

Mmmm. Roses.

*(Witheringly)* How original.

*(Pochsy replaces the card. It slides down the shell and onto the slag. Pochsy points her toes.)*

I was at a friend's funeral a couple of weeks ago? I was a little bit late – I guess I missed about the first ten minutes or so, so I didn't really get what was going on.

At the party afterwards, her parents were weeping over the open casket, which was dripping with pale pink roses and baby blue forget-me-nots. And I felt so bad for them. I mean, didn't they know? *(Pause.)* Pastels are passé.

Flowers come and flowers go, but this season the sunflower is a celebration of life. I myself was carrying a dazzling bouquet, and when I went up to say goodbye to her, I laid it down on her folded arms ... and I pushed all of the other flowers onto the ground.

*(Pause.)*

I forget what was wrong with her. Something about consumption. *(Pause.)* It's okay, though – don't feel bad for me. I don't need her any more.

*(Pause.)*

Excuse me.

*(She dials the telephone.)*

Yes, I would like to make a call and charge it to my room, please? ... Room 90210. *(She winks at the audience.)* 1-976-T-A-L-K.

*(She smiles at the audience as she waits. Then another phone chat theme plays that is both cheesier and dreamier than the last.)*

Hi, my name's Pochsy. I'm five foot seven, I have long, curly blonde hair, and I weigh about, um ... sixty pounds. I was just wondering if anybody out there wants to 'talk'? Oh – and *(spontaneously)* I'm spontaneous.

*(She waits for a significantly shorter period than the last time.)*

Hello? ... Yes, it is. What's your name? ... Oh, hello, 'Dick' ... What do I 'like'? *(bewildered)* Well ... the smell of burning wood makes me wist– *(She is interrupted.)* Oh, you mean, what do I 'think' about?

*(The phone chat music shifts radically into something soaring and romantic.)*

I think about the day when we will fly terror-driven into each other's arms. You will try to put roses in my cheeks, but you will try in vain. Then, as I lie wilting in your arms, faint with love, with just one kiss, you'll take me away from all of this.

Why? What do you … 'think' about?

*(She listens with disgust.)*

Oh!

*(She hangs up abruptly and stares at the receiver for a moment.)*

*(To the audience, revolted)* You don't want to know.

*(She drags her receiver hand across the shell, as though to wipe something from it. Lighting shift: as though a cloud has passed across the sun. Pochsy watches the shift. Pause.)*

Last night I was feeling a little bit lonely and blue. So I went down to the cocktail lounge. The Love Lounge. There was a huge lineup – hundreds of guests, their droopy shorts hanging between their pig legs *(she shudders)*. I just didn't think I could take standing in line for an hour, so I marched right up to the front of the line and I started to cry.

I told them I wasn't feeling well. And so they let me in.

*(Love Lounge music in: a hybrid of Motown and drum and bass.)*

The place was jammed. Everybody was just rubbing up against each other. And everybody was beautiful.

All the guys were wearing loose-fitting jeans, and the girls – you could see their underwear through their dresses. They weren't even conscious of it.

I walked up to a long counter and rested against it. People were sliding condiments to each other. Someone threw a burger onto a plate and slid it to me. It was juicy and sizzling, on a golden bun. It just said, 'Eat me.' And so I did.

*(As though in a burger ad)* Mmmmm.

I drifted past a series of pool tables, and a beach ball landed at my feet. I tossed it to a girl who looked at my outfit and smiled at me. I asked her where the dance floor was. She pointed across the swimming pool. So I walked across the deep end, and when I was almost at the other side, a bottle thrust its way up through the ice. Clean. Clear. It just said, 'Drink me.' And so I did.

*(As though in a 7-Up ad)* Aaaah …

The dance floor was jammed. So I dragged myself up a trellis of sunflowers and onto the balcony level where I could watch.
      *(Timorous)* Just watch.
      A slow song came on, and everybody melted together. A swaying sea of flaccid forms draped damply over one another – I couldn't take my eyes off it.
      It made me feel … wistful.

*(Over the following scene, the lights gradually focus in around Pochsy.)*

Then, behind me, I heard a dull thud. There was a sliding glass door that led out onto a terrace. I went to it, noticed my reflection in the cracked glass, and stepped outside.
      At my feet, there lay a huge white bird. Twitching.
      I kneeled down beside it and said, 'What are you? *(Beat.)* Blind?'

It turned its face up to me. Its eyes were milky. Creamy. It was the face of a man.

The face of an angel.

He reached an arm out to me. I asked him if this had anything to do with the little girl on the plane. He didn't seem to know what I was talking about, so I felt much better about myself, and helped him onto a deck chair. He was barely alive. And he was barely dressed.

He folded his wings behind him and rolled over onto his side. He apologized for the disturbance and said something about having had 'a little too much sun.' I said, 'Who hasn't? If you can't stand the heat, *(she whispers)* get out of the kitchen.'

And he turned his face up to me, opened his cloudy eyes and said, 'You're the one that I want.'

I told him I was spontaneous and outgoing but a little bit shy, and that I would like to get to know him better. I invited him into the Love Lounge for a dance and a drink.

He said that he feared to tread there.

I led him to the fire escape, and we helped each other down to the bottom. In the alley, he tripped and stumbled and leaned up against a dumpster. I lifted the tips of his wings up out of the garbage juice, then I brushed his fine blonde hair back off his face. And it came off in my hands.

I moved closer to him and let my dress caress the tops of his thighs. I made a move to kiss him, but he said, 'No. Not here. Not like this.' *(Pause.)* So I took him back to my hotel room.

I put the 'Do Not Disturb' sign on the door, and laid him down on my comforter. He was shaking all over. I rubbed Intensive Care into his feet and anointed his head with Après Soleil. I told him I was attractive and healthy and not afraid to try new things, and he said, 'Thine is the kingdom, the power and the glory.'

*(She laughs uneasily.)*

We chatted about this and that, and then he said, 'Pochsy, we can talk all night, but that ain't getting us nowhere.' And he sat up and took me in his arms and wrapped his wings around me. And when we kissed ... oooh ... I felt all the wilderness rush through me.

*(She wraps her arms around herself.)*

He ran his hands along my legs and up under my dress. And I ran my hands up under his dress, and pushed it up to the tops of his thighs. *(She pushes the skirt of her own bathing costume up.)* The hairs on his thighs were burnt and brittle, and when I touched them, they blew away. I smelled sulphur.

He rolled over on top of me, *(shy)* and I felt his ... urgency pressed up against me. And his heart beat next to mine. And his dress fell away, and his skin fell like petals around me.

*(She lies back on the shell. The light is now very bright on her, and the stage around her is in blackness. Her hands flutter through the air.)*

I ran my hands up over his ribs to where the wing bones connected to the shoulder blades. And when he kissed my cheek, I heard the cherubs sing.

My fingers traced the arc of his wing bones, to the joint, and down along the smaller connecting bones. I felt the membrane under his feathers. And when he kissed my neck, the wind blew open all the doors.

*(She turns upside down and begins to slide down the shell, squirming in ecstasy.)*

And as he came unto me, I dug my fingers deep into him, and heard the cracking of small bones. And as he came unto me, I knew that, just this once, reality was the best fantasy of all. And that nothing would ever be the same again. And as he came unto me, he whispered in my ear, 'Hail, Pochsy, full of Grace, blessed art thou, and blessed is the fruit of thy womb.'

And I whispered into his ear.

'Oh, baby.'

*(She writhes and tumbles down the shell. There is a bright flash of light and a terrible crash. She lies motionless in the slag and just stays like that for a moment.)*

*(Very soft)* And then he died in my arms. And all of him fell away, and blew away.

*(sfx: wind)* And I sat down beside myself and cried.

*(Music under, Pochsy sings 'Oh, baby' with deep and actual feeling.)*

Your love was heaven sent, oh darling, this I know.
Now what am I supposed to do?
Take my lips, I don't need them,
Take my heart, it's barely beating,
I just lost my mind over you.

Oh, I would heave a sigh for you,
I'd hang my head and cry,
But that's no comfort for a love
Like I will never have again.
And I would surely die for you
If only I believed
That I would see you in heaven.

Oh, oh, whoa-oa, baby, tell me,
How am I supposed to lay me down to sleep,
Without you to help me through the night?
I would surely die for you
If only I believed
That I would see you in heaven.

*(The final chord lingers, unresolved. She speaks.)*

*(Wistfully)* Well, better dead than with somebody else.
    I just don't think I could take that.

*(The chord resolves. Lights shift to a beautiful moonlight state. Pochsy slumps against the shell. Then she turns away from the audience, walks up to the top of the shell, sits down with her back to the audience, picks up the phone and dials.)*

Yes, I'd like to make a collect call please. Area code 911 ...
555 ... H-O-M-E.

*(She listens.)*

Pochsy.

*(Beat.)*

*(Over-enunciating)* Poch-sy.

*(Beat.)*

*(Nasty)* P-O-C-H-S-Y, how do you think it's spelled?

*(Very heavy sigh.)*

Thank you.

*(She peeks at the audience. She tucks a bit of bandage behind her ear.)*

*(Little gasp)* Oh! Hi, it's me. Could you put Mom on the line, too?
*(As she waits, she smiles at the audience.)* Oh– hi, you guys – listen,
I was just calling because …

*(She takes a deep breath.)*

I was wondering if you two recognize the fact that everything
bad that's happened in my life has been your fault?

*(She listens.)*

Oh, good. Okay, I was just checking.
*(She goes to hang up.)*

Oh! Um, can I have your MasterCard number?

*(She grabs a pen which materializes from a crevice, and writes the number on the shell.)*

Expiry date?... Oooh! *(She writes very quickly.)* Okay, thanks.

*(She goes to hang up again.)*

Oh! And, um, *(very softly)* I love you.
*(She hangs up. She sits for a moment, still with her back turned. Then she rises and walks very slowly down the seashell's slope.)*

After the angel died, I was feeling a little bit funny. There were butterflies in my stomach. So I went for a walk along the beach.

*(She steps onto the slag.)*

I walked past the lifeguard who lay sleeping in his chair. I walked past Hazel, collecting seashells in the moonlight. I walked for miles, until I was on shaky ground and the sand gave way beneath my feet.

*(A pretty, trippy melody begins to creep in under the scene.)*

The beach curved around into a little blue lagoon, where the flora grew right down to the water's edge. There was everything there. Prayer plants, impatiens, *(very softly)* forget-me-nots. The water was frothy and teeming with sea creatures. Two-foot minnows leapt high in the air, and little cod paddled by on their backs.

*(She sits down at the edge of the slag.)*

I sat down at the water's edge and listened to the wind in the Dutch elms, and the whippoorwills hollering in the sky.

Then I saw, at my knees, a little sunfish draped over a piece of coral that had washed up. The little fish was panting – exhausted, I suppose, from its fight against the undertow. So I placed it in my lap and stroked its little fin, then I rocked it in my arms until it fell to sleep.

*(With growing pleasure)* I lay down on a bed of narcissi and watched as hundreds of maple keys spiralled down and centrifugally forced their way into the ground. Little sprouts poked from their bulbs and into the sand, and little ants came along and pulled them down deeper. I pulled one out – the little green sprout had branched off into tender little tentacles. I couldn't believe it. So I pulled up another one And another, and another – they were all like that! *(astounded)* Every last one of them.

*(The music grows fuller and more playful, and Pochsy grows more exuberant.)*

High up in the trees, penguins perched and fluttered in amongst the pumpkins that hung down, their stems rakishly askew, like berets. And far out in the lagoon, a Louisiana beaver floated by, carrying an olive branch.

Then the northern lights came on!

*(Sound and lighting shifts.)*

Slowly, at first – they seemed so close *(the lights begin to dance around her)*, it was as if I could reach out and touch them. And I wished I had someone to share this moment with. But I knew, somehow, that I was not alone.

I turned around, and there, on the beach, were fifty … sixty polar bears, drinking Cokes! Further down the beach I saw a couple of spotted Jersey cows, lapping at the saltwater that crystallized on their fuzzy lips and sparkled in the moonlight. There was a soft rustling in the underbrush, and dozens of little pink bunnies marched out. The northern lights started to dance and the bears got all excited, and oohed and aahed, and clapped, and the bunnies started banging on their drums ...

And the cows sang songs of oppression.

*(Pochsy falls to her knees on the slag to pray.)*

*(Cheerfully)* Ow.

Dear Lord,

Thank You for all on this earth that is holy and good. For us two-leggeds sharing with the four-leggeds, and all the wings of the earth, and all green things. For these are the children of one mother, and their father is one spirit.

*(She sings 'Seasick Fish.')*

> Though the fish may all grow seasick,
> Birds be blinded by the light,
> They will fly to Thee more swiftly
> Through the hole in the night.
>
> Though Your tears do sear my flesh,
> I know they're Heaven's calamine,
> For the terrible is beautiful
> And everything's divine.

My heart had grown dull, dear Lord, and my eyes had closed, and my ears had grown heavy of hearing. But I see Your spirit in everything now, for You have slipped through the opening in the sky and You are in everything – visible and invisible – as pure and precious as a snowflake. *(beatific)* In July.

I hear the babies crying,
But, Lord, I'm not afraid.
I know manna falls more easily
When skies are torn away.

And Your spirit moves in everything,
So I'm in ecstasy.
I feel wings of seven butterflies
Beat wildly

*(She gasps. Her fingers flutter over her stomach.)*

You're in me.

The weather continues to be unusually perfect, and the
mosquitoes are all but gone.

*(She winks.)*

Thanks.
Love, Pochsy.

*(She blows God a kiss and swoons, horribly. She looks at the audience
for a moment. She traces her fingers over her head bandage and tucks
stray bits behind her ears.)*

*(Pochsy looks across at the picnic basket. It is suddenly lit up in a shaft
of white light. August, ritualistic music plays under. She crawls, with
excruciating discomfort, across the slag to the picnic basket. She
throws the little gauze blanket aside and pulls out a large bottle of
clear liquid. She holds it up to the sky.)*

Life.

*(She places the bottle down on the slag, then reaches into the basket again, pulls out a disturbingly rubbery fish and holds it up to the sky.)*

Death.

*(She lays the fish beside the bottle, reaches back into the basket and hoists high a big bowl of maraschino cherries.)*

Eternity.

*(Pochsy performs the following 'Fish Ritual' with tremendous gravity: she crosses her chest as though in a Cross-Your-Heart Bra ad, eats a cherry, kisses the fish and tosses it into the water with a splash. She waits to see if the fish swims. It doesn't. She shakes the bottle for a long, long time, till the liquid inside gets very frothy. Then as she uncaps it, all light goes to black except a black light, which makes the liquid glow: intensely fluorescent. It sprays far and wide, like a magical fountain. Lights restore, and she drinks from the bottle.)*

Aaah.

*(She leaps back up onto the seashell, fortified. She throws her arms wide.)*

The world is my oyster. I shall not want.

*(She looks at the cherries and the bottle on the slag, then looks at the audience.)*

I'd offer you some … but it's mine.

*(She sits. She gazes at the audience for a moment.)*

I have to leave tomorrow, so this morning I went down to the beach to collect some seashells. They were fresh out. So I dove into the water where I found some nestled in the thick seaweed. I pulled them out, pried them apart with my perfect white nails, tore out the little sea creatures … and let them swim free.

They didn't come back to me, so I guess they weren't mine to begin with *(little sigh)*.

Then I took all the shells back to my hotel room, where I wrapped them in a soft white towel and placed them in the false bottom of my suitcase.

What didn't fit, I left for Hazel.

*(She picks up phone and dials 0.)*

Yes, I would like to make a call and charge it to my room please? ... Room 649 ... 1-976-l-o-v-e.

*(Insanely cheesy romantic music in.)*

Hi. My name's Pochsy. I'm seven foot nine, I have long, curly, healthy-looking, shiny blonde hair, and I weigh about, um, seventeen pounds. I was just wondering if there's anybody out the– Hello? ... Yes, it is. What's your name? ... Oh *(she glances at the audience)*, hello, 'Harry.' *(She listens for a moment.)* Yes. *(She takes a breath.)* I think I would like to have an intimate conversation.

*(She listens. Then, quietly:)* What's my wildest fantasy? ... My ... my wildest fantasy?

*(Music out. She drops the receiver. Her fingers flutter over her stomach. She looks at the audience and speaks very quietly.)*

I would like to have a baby. That looks just like me ... only littler. With ten little fingers and ten little toes, and soft pink skin that looks and behaves just like fresh young skin.

At night, we will have supper together. Chicken wings for me, marinated in Memories of Babylon, and Decadent Baby Food for her. And when we're all done, we will pull the bones apart, and make a wish.

*(She sings 'Blue Skies.')*

> For happiness
> And pretty things, *(she clutches her stomach)*
> Hushabye, my baby, hear the angels sing,

They're singing, 'Blue skies,
Blue skies forever.'

*(She speaks over the continuing music.)*

After supper, I will dress her up in her little sleepers and bathe her in the cathode rays. Then I will lay down her sweet head and switch on the little intercom – just in case. Then I will make my bed.
And lie in it.

Close your eyes,
Your soul will keep,
But if you die before you wake you know I'll weep,
So dream of blue skies,
Blue skies forever.

When she's a little older, she will bring her friends home to play after school. I will be nice to them, high on the scent of fresh-cut flowers. They will all play outside, in their little sunglasses, making angels in the sand. Hot buttered children on a hot and humid November day. A day so warm the clouds couldn't form even if they wanted to.

*(She does a little soft-shoe down the slope of the seashell.)*
The sun will rise
And melt the skies,
A whole new world that you won't recognize,
Under blue skies,
Blue skies forever.

When she's a teen, she will become a dairy princess, because of her strong bones and teeth and her ability to go all day.
When the time comes, we will move further north, where the wheat still grows. She'll work for Mercury Packers, in the

new branch plant. And she will be exalted. At night she'll come home from work and we will sit on the front stoop and watch the icebergs float south and listen to the penguins crying way up high.

And every ocean will have a silver lining.

*(Pochsy dances back up to the top of the shell, twirling and holding her head, exhilarated. Then she throws her arms wide.)*

> Little girl,
> Ocean pearl.
> Everything is beautiful in this brave new world.
> And we'll have blue skies,
> Blue skies forever,
> And ever,
> And ever,
> And ever,

And ever.

*(She holds her stomach)* Ooh!

*(Blackout.)*

**The End**

*(Post show/curtain call music: 'It's the End of the World as We Know It.')*

# Citizen Pochsy
## Head Movements of a Long-Haired Girl

## Performance History

*Citizen Pochsy: Head Movements of a Long-Haired Girl* was first presented in a public workshop by Pochsy Productions at The Space in Toronto in December 2002. It then premiered at One Yellow Rabbit's High Performance Rodeo in Calgary in January 2003. Subsequent productions were presented by the KaBOOM Festival in Edmonton, Ruby Slippers and the Fire Hall in Vancouver, and by Magnetic North in Ottawa.

Pochsy: Karen Hines
The Musician: Greg Morrison

Text, lyrics and melodies by Karen Hines
Music and sound by Greg Morrison
Directed by John Turner
Stage design by Darren O'Donnell
Lighting by Cimmeron Eve Meyer
T-shirts by Peter Moller
SuperVision by Sandra Balcovske

At the time of publication, *Citizen Pochsy* is still touring, and will have its first full production at One Yellow Rabbit's Big Secret Theatre.

### Set

The set consists of four chairs in a row and an electric or baby grand piano. If the piano is electric, it is a Yamaha, with all the letters blacked out except the 'HA.' The piano is stage left, the chairs just off centre, to stage right.

The establishing props include: a standard banker's box, a knapsack, a Starbucks paper take-away bag, a Starbucks coffee cup (grande) and a paper chit from a take-a-number roll.

The Starbucks bag contains three bottles of Spirit Water (Starbucks' exclusive brand). The knapsack contains four emptied and crushed bottles of Spirit Water, a hairbrush, liquid paper, a pen, scissors, a few loose documents, antibacterial wipes, lip balm, a vial of aromatherapy, a number of crumpled plastic bags and candy wrappers, a cellphone and car keys (unseen: there only for the sound effect).

The contents of the banker's box are more mysterious.

### Costume

Pochsy wears a knitted black toque and stylish black leather boots solid enough for factory work. She begins the show in a fuzzy knitted white sweater-coat, with a rainbow-striped scarf and matching gloves.

As the show progresses, she strips off layer after layer, revealing first a miniskirt and a teal blue hoodie, then layered T-shirts sporting the names and logos of 'Mercury Packers' and 'Lead World.'

In the crook of her right arm, there is a brilliant white cotton swab held with adhesive tape: the kind of band-aid you get when you have given blood, or had it taken.

**Makeup**

Pochsy's face is ivory white. Her lips are blood red. There is a little purple around her very thick-lashed kohl-smudged eyes.

Hair: excellent, auburn and long.

*(As the audience enters, there is a sound recording of Buddhist monks chanting. Once the audience is in, a bald man in a very hip T-shirt enters and sits at the piano. As he begins to play a sad melody, the monks and house lights fade. Soft, soothing lights bathe the waiting-room chairs. After a moment, Pochsy enters from the same place the audience has entered from. She is carrying a banker's box, a knapsack and a Starbucks bag. She does not see the musician. The coffee is balanced on top of the box. She puts her knapsack and the Starbucks bag on the chairs and sips her coffee. She looks around and sees the audience. She puts the banker's box right in the middle of the stage, downstage of the chairs. A soft-edged spotlight comes up about seven paces to her right. She moves into it, looks at the audience and smiles at them.)*

POCHSY: Um ...

A few weeks ago, on an ordinary day, in the middle of the day, I was at work and ... I was feeling a bit discombobulated. I dunno, I've just been super-busy lately – just ... super-busy – and plus I had just gotten a speeding ticket that morning and also I had just given blood and plus I had just switched over to a new long-distance program so I was kind of all, you know, *('crazy' noise) glagghghgh*, and anyway –

*(She takes a breath.)*

I got paged on my break. To answer the phone. It was the government calling.

*(Pause.)*

They say that it's random. Being audited. They say it can happen to anyone. At any time.

And I do understand that I am a citizen of this country and everything, but I mean, yes and no: *(irritated)* I never even vote.

*(The spotlight fades quickly. Pochsy notices it fade. Another spotlight appears on the opposite side of the stage. She walks into it.)*

I was talking to my friend at work the other day? Sari? And we were just talking about our lives, and our jobs, and me-e-eaning – you know, just coffee-break stuff. And Sari started comparing her life to this other girl we both know there: Angie, who is a ... mmmm, oh, what is that? – a bitch.

And I told Sari not to feel so down. That Angie might have a better job than her – more friends, more job security, nicer clothes – but I said, 'Sari, you've got kids who love you and who you've brought into this world and looked after. So what if you're not as young any more? Yeah, Angie's got a great body, but you've got the body of a mother, who has delivered two  gorgeous, healthy children. What's Angie done? Really?

And we both just stood there for a moment.

*(She smiles and just stands there for a moment.)*

Then Sari said, 'I don't have any kids ... ' *(She rolls her eyes.)* And I realized I was thinking of my other friend at work – Melissa!

*(She sighs.)*

*(Softly)* I didn't know what to say then. What that might mean. About me-e-eaning.

*(She steps into a new pool of light, centre stage.)*

For a while I was really into the whole Buddhist thing. But then who wasn't, right? Who didn't want to join the movement away from egotism and toward the deeper meaning of life that lies beneath intellect … *(dryly)* in the nineties?

I am still searching for a deeper level of meaning and blahd-edyblah, I'm just not so obsessed by the whole pursuit-of-Nirvana part of it: I've moved beyond that now.

At a certain point you realize: you can go on endlessly searching for the perfect faith, and these days, in this world, I just don't think there is such a thing. So now I'm searching for a way to marry Eastern philosophy with more North American ideals. In a way that has almost NOTHING to do with intellect.

You just have to figure it out.

For example: when you go to yoga class? I don't think there's anything wrong with wearing something super-tight. And a little fresh lipstick never killed anybody.

*(Beat.)*

Well … Anybody human.

*(She casts down her eyes.)*

So, I guess I'm sort of a Neo-Buddhist. Or … Post-Buddhist more.

*(Pause.)*

All I know for certain is, I just wanna live long enough to be young and beautiful … forever.

*(Music in under.)*

My name is Pochsy. And this is my story.

(*Music to full: a bouncy, poppy, exuberant girl song. Pochsy climbs atop her banker's box and dances go-go. She sings 'Centre of the Universe.'*)

> Take my hand, let's blow this land
> Of be-or-not-to-be.
> Come dive into the Centre
> Of the Universe with me.
> I won't let the bad bugs bite;
> We'll shuck the oysters, pluck the pearls,
> And I will be your Centre …

(*She tosses her hair over her shoulder.*)

> Of the Universal Girl.

(*Pochsy seems confused by her own weird lyric for a moment. Then she shrugs and speaks.*)

Every morning, in the morning, I wake up to an achingly brilliant sun. Though I've been asleep for hours, my breath is minty fresh, so I know it's going to be a good day.

Every morning, in the morning, I trace my fingers over the thick morning paper, slide out the entertainment section, and just … push the rest away.

My name is Pochsy: Taxpayer. Working girl.

(*She twirls on the banker's box, almost falls off, then continues dancing and singing.*)

This flight is inward bound,
The dust is swirling all around,
We're diving through a brand-new stratosphere.
But if the sky falls down,
We'll dive below this shaky shaky ground
And baby I will whisper
Soft sweet nothings in your ear.

I'm calling to you, the apple's seedless, take a bite.
Just take my hand and I'll take you there tonight.

Every morning, in the morning, I step into the shower and wash and repair my damaged hair. I glide cool steel across my milky calves and watch my blood swirl down the drain, where it will mingle with the blood from a billion other calves.

Every morning, I drink a glass of orange juice made from oranges that have been infused with genes from the bones of small monkeys for a higher concentration of calcium, half the fat, and twice the fun!

My name is Pochsy: SIN number 555 555 55, um ... 5!

I'm calling to you, my dream is waking, wild and true.
Just take my hand, and my dream might be of you.

Every morning I step outside and I grab a steaming Ethiopian.

*(Music halts. She clarifies.)*

Coffee!

*(Music restores.)* Then I slide in behind the wheel of my new Pontiac Impatience. I power-lock the crumple-proof doors, and,

as I cut off the bitch in the silver Infiniti, I gaze into my rearview mirror and I imagine a beautiful future.

'Cuz I believe that every day is a day when nothing has to happen, but anything could! I believe what could be should be. I believe there are no errands – just chances to drive!

Every morning, in the morning, I hear a voice whisper, 'It's okay, Pochsy. Everything's going to be okay.' I recognize the voice. I recognize the sound. It is the sound of my own voice. *(She grins.)* I love that sound.

My name is Pochsy: Citizen of the World.

> We'll save the day and spend the night
> Making two and two make five.
> I'm calling to you.
> I'm calling to you.
> We'll muddle through from nine till nine.
> And if I never change my mind,
> I'll be yours and you'll be mine.
> I'm calling to you.
> I'll be your cuddly Columbine,
> I'll be your Fraulein Frankenstein,
> I'll be your calming calamine,
> I'll be yours if you'll be mine.

*(She gazes right into the eyes of a single audience member.)*

> I'm calling to you.

*(She winks at the audience member, then switches to another.)*

> I'm calling to you.

*(She smiles, bewitchingly, then switches to another.)*

I'm calling to you.

*(She extends her arms out to the whole audience and smiles.)*

I'll be yours if you'll be mine.

*(Pochsy tosses her hair. The song ends, she steps down from the box and light floods the stage. She looks at the waiting room chairs, then walks down toward the front of the stage, close to the audience.)*

They say, in Buddhist *(she corrects herself)* –mmmm, 'If you want to know what you were doing in the past, look at your body now. But if you want to know what will happen to you in the future, look at what your *mind* is doing now.'

*(Pause. She peers into the eyes of the patrons in the front rows, then giggles nervously and backs away from them.)*

When I think about the future, I try to have a beautiful feeling about the world and to project that feeling out. To shine love in all directions, which I believe is our ultimate purpose in this life.

*(Pause.)*

But I was in a restaurant the other night? Just grabbing some salad, and some Asian-Style McNuggets – which are made with real chicken, now, by the way – and anyway, I heard these people talking about this concept that the soul is actually just that: a concept. That we invented. Humans. And evolved over time through all the human virtues like mercy and honour, through language and art. The creative impulse.

That because we invented the soul, we are, therefore, capable of dismantling it. Through opposite forces. Over time.

*(Pause.)*

Which made me feel better in a way. Because, if our souls were never really real, then they were never really there to begin with. And like they say, if you love something, set it free. If it comes back, it's yours. If it doesn't, you don't have to feel bad about it. Or something ... I don't have the exact wording but ... *(She slips her fingers up inside her toque, traces them over her temples, then tucks a few stray strands of hair behind her ears.)*
Sorry, I've been super-busy lately so my brain's a bit of a sieve.

*(She removes her white coat, revealing her tight little hoodie and miniskirt. She drapes the coat over a chair, notices the audience still looking at her and smiles coyly.)*

I work at Mercury Packers. Where I pack mercury.
It's right across the street from my house, which is great for me because it only takes me a minute. To drive.
Parking's a bit of a bitch and adds at least five or ten, but what can you do? And plus, I get five bucks off the chit with my voucher, so how can you NOT drive? It's just one of the perks.

*(Pause.)*

I work inhuman hours. Very inhuman. But then, they're set by humans so I guess they're human hours. Very human. But it's a good job. Two weeks vacation. Every year. Great cafeteria. And it's super-safe. Now.
Since the filters.

*(She pulls a bottle of water from her Starbucks take-away bag.)*

I have lots of friends. Work friends mostly. All. So, I don't know if that counts. But some of them I would be friends with outside of work. Probably. Like when you have friends from high school. Which I don't have. Any more. Used to, but *ghghghghhhh (she shudders)*.

But I would say that, as of now, I have four friends. Or – two, really. Ish. Well, one, really. Ish. But they say that one good friend is all you actually need in this world, and I have that.

Ish.

*(She drinks some water.)*

Anyway, at Mercury Packers, they switched a few years ago and now we're all considered self-employed. Private contractors to Mercury Packers. It works better for me 'cuz it gives me a little more wiggle room on my taxes, and it works better for them because they don't have to pay any benefits, which they explained in the incoherent brochure that outlined the new taxation structure. It sounds complicated but it's actually very simple:

They don't get audited; I do.

I don't know, it's the first time I'm dealing with it all, so it's a little confusing …

*(She looks offstage right, into the blackness. Then, conspiratorially:)*

I get a bit of a weird vibe from the people who work here. The 'government employees.' Like, *(she looks off right again)* when I got here today, I tried to tip the girl at the Information desk, but apparently I was being déclassé, and I'm, like, excuse me, I've never actually *been* audited before; I don't *know* the tipping protocols.

Then, after Information, they send you through Security, which is a total joke. *(She pulls a pair of scissors out of her knapsack and snips at the air.)*

Then you go upstairs to Collections Reception, where the commissionaire gave me my number – or, rather *(she disgustedly holds up a chit with her nails)*, he licked his fingers and gave me my number. I said, 'Tha-hha-nkkyou!' *(said as a cough, then she subsequently adds a second, more focused and pointed cough).*

Then he tells you to go to a certain waiting room.

*(She puts the chit down, then wipes her fingers with an antibacterial wipe.)*

This waiting room.

*(She wipes the chit with the antibacterial wipe.)*

As opposed to if you're here for GST or child tax credit, in which case they direct you to some other waiting room. *(She continues wiping her fingers.)* Or if you're filing for a deceased person, in which case I don't know what room you're in and I don't want to know that.

*(She crumples the antibacterial wipe. She wanders in search of a trash can.)*

They say that it's random. Being audited. But I think it's because I was late with last year's return. I told them it was my accountant's fault. They requested my accountant's name. I gave them my sister's name – not that she was my accountant, just … I thought they might want to look at her books and records first.

*(She crosses way upstage looking for a trash can.)*

I asked if I could have more time to organize my files. They said I shouldn't need any time so long as all my income had been declared and my expenses were properly accounted for.

*(Chilly silence.)*

I tried to explain the paradox of making me come in to ostensibly make me pay more tax while simultaneously denying me the opportunity to go to work to earn money to pay tax *on* ... but they didn't seem to understand my position. Which might have had something to do with the fact that they spoke English as a *fifth* language.

*(Another chilly silence.)*

I suggested that as a possibility. They suggested the possibility of going back a few more years. Like seven. More. Years. And you quickly realize: *(sotto voce)* they can do anything they want. This isn't about ethics any more.

It's wa-a-ay deeper than that.

*(She looks around.)*

You organize your books and records, and you go in. Come in. To this waiting room. Here.

*(She sits.)*

When you ask how long it will be, they say they don't know. And you quickly realize: they don't know.

*(She drapes her arm across the chair beside her. She dangles the antibacterial wipe from her baby finger. Seductively, she unzips her hoodie with her other hand, revealing her Mercury Packers T-shirt beneath.)*

I'm hoping I won't be here all day, *(minxy)* which is why I'm in my work clothes. In case I can go in for part of my shift.

*(She drops the antibacterial wipe on the floor. She casually looks the other way, smooths her hair and drinks some water.)*

But in a way, it's good. Like they say, freedom comes with responsibility. It's just part of being a citizen. Like voting. Like shovelling your walk. Like not littering. Like declaring all your purchases at the border. Like disposing of your batteries in the correct way *(flicker of confusion)*. Like coming to a totally complete stop at stop signs.

    Like giving blood.

*(She reaches into her knapsack and rummages. She pulls out a small vial and unscrews the lid, then sniffs the vial.)*

But I don't think I have anything to worry about. I mean, what are they going to get from me? I'm just a working girl with a modest weekly income. *(She sniffs the vial.)* Very modest. *(She sniffs the vial.)* So I know I shouldn't be scared. It's just …

    I have this little dress on layaway. The one I saw at Kinderslut. The one I try on every day at lunch. *(She sniffs.)* Makes me feel five.

*(She sniffs deeply from the vial. She notices the audience noticing it.)*

Don't worry. It's nothing weird. *(She pops the vial in her pocket.)* It's for … um …

*(She furrows her brow. She reaches into her pocket, then reads the vial's label.)*

'Clarity.'

*(She traces the fingers of one hand over a temple and tucks stray bits of hair behind her ear. All lights fade around her except one small, cold light that shines on her from out and above. She looks up and into it. She clasps her hands.)*

Dear God,
 Please protect me from evil. Please deliver me from peril. Please give me the courage and strength to face this Godforsaken day.

*(Beat.)*

I'm sorry. I didn't mean 'God' forsaken. I meant ... I don't know what I meant—

*(The light snaps to black. Another cold, small light comes up across the stage. She moves into it.)*

Dear God,
 Please forgive me for all the evil and weak things I have done in my life. Please forgive me for all the people whom I have hurt, and grant them the strength, and the wisdom – and the Clarity – to forgive me, too.
 And for those people who would hurt me, please, Lord, just... use Your instincts. Presuming You have instincts, which might be seen as more, um, animal. Which – I dunno if that's an insult, 'animal.' Or if perhaps suggesting that 'animal' is insulting might be the greater crime. Sin. Seeing as animals are, of course, beautiful. Just as all nature is, and, in fact, at times more beautiful than many humans, depending on the species of animal or ... plant. Or the specific haircut any given human might be sporting at that particular point ...

*(Pause.)*

I'm sorry. Strike this prayer.

Can one actually delete *(the light snaps out)* – a prayer?

*(A new cold, small spotlight comes up down centre. Pochsy crawls into it.)*

*(Tentatively)* Dear Lord,

Please give me courage and strength. On this day. In this world. This world which is a frightening place, no offence.

I just need to feel Your love.

Not that I'm saying You haven't been loving me. I just haven't been feeling it. So if You have been loving me, no problem. But if You haven't ... maybe You could think about why. Or You could just meditate on why. Or whether. And when I say 'You' I say it ('You') with a capital Y.

*(Pause.)*

Just let me know if there's anything I should do. *(She thinks for a second.)* Or, You know, don't let me know – I'll just have, um, faith. I'll just figure something else out.

*(Pause.)*

But then we Both know where that can lead, don't we? Your detachment? My hurt? *(She arches an eyebrow.)* Other gods ... ?

Not that I'm threatening. I don't mean to send any mixed messages. But then, You know Yourself how easy it is to fall into that: 'Mixed Messages.' The 'Whether or Not' thing. It's just ... You might want to observe how it makes *You* feel. *(condescending)* And I don't mean to criticize 'You.' It's not Your fault.

*(Pause.)*

Well ... it is and it isn't, right?

*(Music in, very light and uplifting, like a phone company ad.)*

I'm just saying, when things don't go so well on any given day, or *(indicating Him)* week, or *(indicating herself)* seven-year period ...
    I'm just saying:

*(Pochsy sings 'One Clear Purpose.')*

> One clear purpose
> Would help to light my way.
> Just one clear purpose
> To navigate the dark of day.
> If You'd provide the road map,
> I would make the sacrifice,
> But one clear purpose
> Would be nice.

*(Her hoodie slips off her shoulders. Her hips move gently with the music.)*

> Just one good reason
> Why I'm lost as I am,

One good reason
I should be Your baby *(teasing)* la-a-amb.
Sometimes faith eludes me,
I believe less than I should –
That's when one good reason
Would be good.

I'm just thinking about the future, really. Your future. There's a lot of confusion in the world and people want something simpler now. A distillation of ideas. A compression of meaning. I guess it's like that whole Michael Douglas/Kirk Douglas thing: which Olsen twin is that? Who is Angelina Jolie's father, again? Is that Luke? Is that Owen? Does it matter?

I think it does.

'Cuz sometimes faith eludes me.
I get You mixed up with Christ.

*(Pochsy strikes a crucifix pose. Her hips move sinuously.)*

That's when one clear icon
Would be ni-i-ice.
Yeah, one clear icon,
One clear purpose,
One good reason would be –

And I won't even get into the whole good and evil thing. As far as I'm concerned: *(sportively)* Don't judge me and I won't judge You.

*(She tosses her hair.)*

Yeah, one clear icon,

One clear purpose,
One good reason would be nice.

Anyway, thanks for Your time. I know
it's infinite, but thanks anyway.

With love,
Your Number-One Fan (small f),
Pochsy.

*(Pochsy blows God a soft kiss, then loses her balance and falls forward
onto her hands. She rolls elegantly to one side and, smoothly, she stands
and starts slinking around the stage. She peels off her hoodie and wraps
it around her waist, revealing her Mercury Packers T-shirt, a longer-
sleeved T-shirt layered underneath it, as well as the brilliant white
band-aid in the crook of her right elbow. She notices the band-aid is
showing and pulls her long sleeve down over it, then smiles demurely
at the audience.)*

When they gave me my appointment, they told me to put aside a
whole day for my audit. Or, sorry – 'reassessment.' That's the
official ... what they call it.

But they didn't tell me how long I'd have to wait for the
actual reassessment procedure, um ... process.

Not that I mind, it's just that *(she says loudly)* I was really
hoping to give blood this afternoon. *(She looks off right, toward the
employees.)*

And plus, I forgot my book.

I've been reading a lot lately. Small stories. About little lives.
Stories that are moving and life-affirming and can be read in
twenty-minute snatches before sleep.

Stories that leave you laughing with a tear in your eye, or
crying with a smile on your lips. Because I like epiphanies. I need

a gentle maxim now and then. I believe the English language is
beautiful and full of grace.

It should not be made to carry a great weight.


But, whatever. *(She opens her pack.)* Sometimes it's good to have
time just to sit with your own thoughts. *(She pulls out her phone.)*
And lately, I've just been so super-busy, *(chirpy)* so this is good.
*(She checks the phone, places it on a chair at a safe distance from the
contaminated chit, stares at it for a moment, then, murderously:)* My
phone doesn't work in here, but this is good. *(She glares stage right,
sniffs some Clarity, then pulls out a second bottle of water and drifts
down, very close to the audience.)*

After the commissionaire gave me my number, I peeked in the
'Interview Room,' and *(she whispers)* the table is in the shape of a
coffin. Or, like, a bullet, more.

And the auditor sits at the flat end, while you sit somewhere
on a curve, and their computer is sunken down into the table and
covered with glass, while your shit spills all over the top of it – it's
like some kind of Freudian feng shui! Some kind of Chinese
water-torture test. *(Beat.)* Though there's no actual water
involved, and *(squirming)* also – I'm sorry, I didn't mean to
say Chinese water torture, I meant more a *German* water...
torture ...

*(She is uncomfortable. )*

You can say 'German,' right?

*(Pause. She drinks some water. She looks at the bottle, then turns it so
that the 'Spirit' label can be read by the audience.)*

They called me in here on my day off. Which is a total drag.
Because I've been trying to work on my day off. But whatever,

really, because at Mercury Packers, they don't even pay you at a higher rate now for overtime. You do make more money, though, but it's just because you work more hours – I know, it sounds simple, but it's actually very complicated and, anyway, it's gotten very political. At Mercury Packers. Ever since they became a subsidiary. Of Lead World.

*(Pause. She drinks some more water.)*

But I'm sorry, I shouldn't go on about work – it's so boring. It's just I'm about to be audited for it, so ...

*(She goes to the chairs and sits down. She places her water bottle on the floor beside the first bottle. She removes some crumpled wrappers, etc., from her knapsack, looks around cursorily for the nonexistent trash can, then places the garbage carefully on a chair. She reaches one arm deep into the knapsack and rummages noisily through it for an amazingly long time, while staring absently at the audience. Then she pulls out a brush.)*

They say we live at at a time of unprecedented danger. But then I think every 'time' has been a time of unprecedented danger, now, hasn't it? I think that's what makes it a 'time.' It has always been this way – er – like – 'thus.'

So if it has always been 'thus' and we're all still here, can't we just relax and have a good 'time'? I mean, what's the worst that can happen? Really? As long as you feel fine about what you've done in your life.

*(She starts brushing her hair.)*

But you know those days when you wake up and you suddenly feel like your whole life has been a meaningless waste? You just feel hopeless and ashamed, because of what you've done, or, you know *(she indicates a specific member of the audience)*, haven't done?

*(She stops brushing her hair.)*

*(To the audience member)* And, when I say 'you,' I don't mean you. Specifically. I meant ... *(gently)* All of you.

*(She resumes brushing.)*

But I think people can stand almost anything, as long as they're not alone. And at a certain point you realize: it doesn't matter what you 'do.' With your 'life.' As long as you know that somewhere, someone loves you. In the end. Which is also why I'm in such a bad mood lately. Not that I don't have love in my life. I do. It's just, I don't have it from the *kind* of people I would best like it from. And I don't think that's a judgemental thing – it's more ... aesthetic.

*(She stops brushing her hair.)*

I think I'm a little bit in love. *(She giggles.)* With a fireman. *(She giggles again.)* With ALL firemen!

    *(Lambent)* I don't know, there's just something about them! And I just have this feeling. So, I haven't been dating as much lately, *(she crosses her fingers and whispers)* just in case! Plus, call me crazy, but there's a fire station right in my neighbourhood and I *don't* think it's a coincidence!

*(She brushes her hair.)*

Anyway, these are just some of the things on my mind. At this 'time.' And so sometimes I can't help but think about all the sad and lonely people who wander through this world and never find that special someone. That person who will melt their heart. That person who they want to be with. For the rest of their lifestyle.

*(She stops brushing, abruptly.)*

Life. I meant life.

*(She goes to put the brush down, but there is no more room on the chair because of all the garbage she has put there. Delicately, she places some of the garbage on the floor beneath the chair, then places the brush on the chair. Then she just looks at the audience for a moment. The lights grow cooler.)*

The other night, in the middle of the night, I woke up and I was feeling a little restless. *(She squirms and rises.)* In my body.

I got up and just started wandering around my room, and I'm, like, what is the *matter* with me?

*(Swiftly)* Is it that the world's population of six billion is poised to grow to ten billion over the next half-century and, in the process, lay waste to many of the ecological communities on which it depends for survival?

*(Beat.)*

But I thought, no-o-o-o-o, that's not it.

So then I thought … *(swiftly)* Is it the problem of existing with the paradox of my condemnation of the violation of human rights abroad when my own precious lifestyle is the result of my own ancestors' nearly identical violation of indigenous peoples

here and, not even by much extension, of my own continuing
violation of all they hold sacred?

*(Beat.)*

But I'm, like, no; I can barely even say that!

*(She paces.)*

It wasn't the melting ice caps, and it wasn't Mad Cow, or avian
influenza, or West Nile, or North Korea, or the number of unex-
ploded warheads in the world, or mould in the schools, or all the
hormones in the chicken, or the Prozac in the rivers, or the child
soldiers of Sierra Leone, or the pa-a-a-nda bear-r-rs.

*(Pause. She thinks about the panda bears for a moment.)*

But I couldn't sleep. So I did some valerian. I did my abs. I exfoli-
ated my skin. I wept for all the dead cells I would never see again!
   *(Hushed)* And then I realized what felt bad in me.
   What my soul was crying for.
   I realized: these are my saving years. And I need a plan that's
right for me!

*(Radical lighting shift.)*

So I went to my bank.

*('Bank' music kicks in: pulsing, urgent.)*

In the blackness of the night,
My branch was lit with a thousand lights.
I saw three tellers at their tills ...

*(She strikes a dance pose and sings.)*

      Whispering on their phones.

*(She jumps up on a chair and dances.)*

      I asked them why they worked so late,
      They offered me new mortgage rates.
      I told them I don't own a home,
      Too scared to buy alone.

I said:

      Rock me in your arms,
      Hold me while I weep.
      I'm your client, I'm your baby,
      Rock me back to sleep.

      They swiped my card, they wiped my eyes,
      These c-reps in white shirts, blue ties.
      One held me close, one stroked my hair,
      One asked me for my PIN.

      I told them 'bout my overdraft,
      Confessed my debts; they washed my hands,
      They had forgiven everything
      The second I walked in.

This was not about the past.
    This was about the future.
    My future.
    This was about me.

114

They said:

> Hushabye, my sweet,
> You know our love is true.
> You're our client, you're our babe,
> We've got a plan that's right for you.

*(She dances across the chairs, accidentally knocking bits of trash off as she goes.)*

> Then another man appeared,
> Golden hair and a golden beard.
> His teeth and tie pin glowed to match
> The sparkles in his eyes.

*(Breathlessly)* He was the Senior Financial Services Manager.

> He asked me if I bank by phone,
> I asked Him will I die alone?
> He asked me for my history,
> Somehow I told Him everything.

I told Him I give blood. I've been on a reserve. I told Him I'm a vegetarian – A partial vegetari–

*(Music out.)*

I only eat veal.

*(Music in. She jumps down off the chairs and moves stealthily downstage.)*

He asked if I give to charities.
> I said all I have to give is love.

He asked if I was married.
I said I don't want to die alone.
He asked if I have children.
I said, 'I don't want to be life-giving.
I want to be breath-*taking*'!

*(Music out.)*

He said, 'Don't worry. You will be.'

*(Music in. She crawls, kitten-like, onto the banker's box.)*

Then I crawled into His lap.

And I said:

> Rock me in your arms,
> Stroke me while I weep.
> You're my Banker, you're my Daddy,
> Rock me till I sleep.

*(She dances provocatively on the box.)*

He asked me what I had in mind.

I asked him about the 'ethical portfolio,' the one that helps the Third World poor. But he could only offer 3.5 percent, which he worked out for me upon his marble desk beside a bible, which fell open to Christ's own words: 'There will be poor always.'

I stared into my Banker's eyes. He stroked me with His hoof. Then He pressed His soft pink lips to my ear and blew a zero deep into the centre of my mind.

There's something in the air
Spinning magic everywhere.
He said, 'Hush, my sweet,
Your transaction's now complete.
Hear the golden calves sing hoodoo prayers!'

*(Briefly, Pochsy dances an erotic hoodoo dance.)*

The customer service representatives emptied my account and transferred all my funds into a plan that's right for me. The

Senior Financial Services Manager pressed his thumb into my third eye and deep inside my pearl-grey brain the zero burst apart and formed six zeroes more.

*(She staggers backwards. The stage is bathed in red light.)*

I fell backwards into the arms of two securities officers, who carried me into a huge vault. The walls were lined with red wet velvet and the floor was covered with earth.

 They laid me down. On 'Solid Ground.'
 Then they rocked me in their arms.
 And zeroes flooded all the pearl-grey coils of my mind.

  Rock me back to sleep …

I don't remember much after that. *(She giggles.)* I don't even remember driving home.

  Rock me back to sleep …

  Rock me back to sleep …

  Rock me back to sleep …

*(Rock 'n' roll light show ending: a strobe sequence during which Pochsy does a James Brown drop to the floor. Between strobe black-outs, she peeks under her band-aid. She presses her temples with her palms. Then she rises, snakes around the room and strikes a saucy pose. Music out.)*

On my thirteenth birthday, I woke up with a pair of the most beautiful breasts I had ever seen.

*(Music in. She snakes around the room again and strikes another pose. Music out.)*

I was walking down the street the other day, and this girl came up to me? And I think she was trying to ask me for directions, but there was something funny about her voice, and something weird with how she walked and something very wrong with her skin.

And then I realized: she was old.

If I ever got old, I would just *die.*

*(Music in. She snakes around and strikes another pose. Music out.)*

For a lot of people, the only thing standing between them and a beautiful future is their imagination. Unconsciously, they create negative situations because they imagine them. Poverty. Loneliness. Crepe neck. So when I think about the future, I like to think about the *(super-sweet)* chilllldrennn. 'Cuz, like, they are the future. The future belongs to the chilllldrennnnn. *(Beat.)* Or, like, *(pregnantly)* to some of them.

*(Lights restore to a more dramatic waiting-room state: there seems to be a vapour in the air through which shards of greenish light shine.*

*Pochsy peels off her Mercury Packers T-shirt, revealing another, tighter, shorter long-sleeved T-shirt beneath it. It has a logo, a green globe surrounded by black rays, at the centre of her chest.*

*She reaches into her knapsack and pulls out a few crumpled wrappers. She looks around, cursorily again, for a trash can, then sees the garbage on the floor, as though for the first time, and tosses the wrappers down with the rest. She reaches into her knapsack again and pulls out two folded documents, which she holds for the rest of the scene.)*

Personally, I'm a little bit ambivalent about the whole baby thing.
Like whether or not I should have one. I guess I'm just more
about myself right now. Like, what's going to happen ... to me?
What do I need? What do I want? Do I need what I want? Do I
want what I need?

*(Pause. She drinks some water.)*

I'm not so big on newborns – I just
find they're so selfish.

But I do like kids.

Like, every time the president
talks about 'your family,' you
know, like taking 'your family' travelling, or Christmas with
'your family,' or making 'your family' feel more secure – than
they are ... in actuality *(she searches)* ... I guess ... *(she stops search-
ing)* I realize I don't have one. A family. A young family. I have
my old family, but *(repulsed) ghaaahhhghhhhh.*

Anyway, I hear the president talk or, you know, other
celebrities, about life, the world, and I just want to go out and
have a kid. They're, like, instant meaning. Meaning in a bonnet.
Little strollers full of meaning.

*(Pause. Over the following scene, the lights focus in around her very,
very gradually.)*

I had a foster child once.

Her name was Azzraj ... mar ... Azzmajran ... *(concen-
trating)* Azzrajumbrazzmmm ... hmmm ... *(She giggles softly.
She gives up.)* I know how to spell it.

I had asked for one of those tiny little children – one of the
ones with the huge brown eyes and the long, wet lashes? They
sent me a picture of this perfect little creature. She was eleven

years old, but she was so-o-o tiny she looked like she was three. So I said yes.

I sent them the money, and I sent her a letter, just telling her a little bit about myself. About my job, and that, though I don't have a lot of money, I wanted to share some of it with her – not just because of karma or – what is that? – compassion (which I had been 'exploring') but because I was seeking to grow less 'attached.' To things. *(smiles coyly)* For my e-e-go-o.

Then she sent me a letter telling me a little bit about herself.

That her father had been shot at her feet as her whole family watched and that her mother had subsequently torn out her own eyes, which meant the little girl and her brother had to go to work in a rug factory, until her brother became ill and that now she had to walk to work all by herself.

*(Pause.)*

I wrote back: 'There are no problems. *(Pause.)* Only challenges.'

*(She smiles, tranquilly.)*

It was nice for a while, but then – I don't know what happened. I just got super-busy. Just … busy. And *(wistful)* we lost touch.

Or – one of my cheques bounced. I think …

*(She stares into space for a moment.)*

I phoned to see if it would affect my credit rating, but they said no. And besides, if it's to a charity, it isn't really bouncing it because you didn't *owe* them the money in the first place!

*(Pause. Little smile.)*

I do like those rugs, though.

Inspired in privation, but rich in the culture and heritage of the children who weave them – a heritage that is expressed in pure wool. With accents of silk.

They're handmade, so they have those little irregularities, you know, like, depending on how the child was fe-e-e-eling. On that day. *(whispers)* Makes them dynamic.

*(Pause.)*

I did keep her letters, though. Both.

In one of them she thanked me for my compassion. She said that she felt blessed. Then she said she had been instructed not to disparage our God. Then she asked what 'blessed' meant. I told her that 'bless' means 'transformation through power.'

*(Beat.)*

In Tibetan.

*(Pause. She switches the documents from one hand to the other and has a drink of water.)*

I do think about her sometimes, Azzrjjmmaj ... Azzrajmarbar ... Azzrajmaibarjram. *(She laughs, sticks out her tongue and shakes her hands in the air.)* Oh, forget it! *(then, radiant)* But I know that childrennn are protected somehow. Like, you know how when kids fall off a bicycle, they practically bounce? Or, like, a snowmobile? *(then, really radiant)* Children are favoured by God. I like to think that God is watching over her. *(She considers this.)* Or Mohammed, I guess. Allah. Whoeverrr. *(sweet smile)* It doesn't matter.

*(Pause. Pochsy shivers.)*

Do you ever get a really empty feeling inside? Like, just suddenly? And you don't know why?

*(Silence.)*

I hate that.

*(Pochsy notices that she is now isolated in a hard spotlight. She steps from it, carefully, and it dissolves into an unsettling combination of footlights and unearthly green tops. She goes to her banker's box and pulls out a rust-red envelope. She puts the two documents she has been holding into the envelope, licks and closes it. She turns away from the audience to reveal, on her back, a huge Lead World logo, with a green globe emanating black rays to match the graphic on her chest. She walks to the chairs, reaches into her knapsack again and pulls out a third document. She sits down.)*

They say it's random, but Angie, the – oh, what was that? the, um, the bitch – Angie said that's just pulling your file. That they don't call you unless they think they found something fishy.

*(She pulls some garbage out of her knapsack, throws it absently onto the floor, then takes out a pen.)*

Then, after they call you, they send you a list of questions that Angie said must be about what they thought they found. Questions about certain business deductions. I told Angie I didn't understand their questions, and could she please help me? Angie suggested I hire an accountant. I reminded Angie I don't make as much as her so I couldn't afford to pay an accountant and doesn't that mean that I am in an unfair position with the government? Angie asked me if I knew that there are one billion people in the world living on less than one American dollar a day which is less than most American families spend to feed their cat.

I said maybe I should get a cat.

*(Icy)* An American cat. Call that cat Freedom. *(Pause.)*

*(Saccharine)* He-e-ere, Fre-e-eedom-m-m ...

*(Pause.)*

The next week I found Angie crying in the ladies' room at lunch. She'd just found out that she was being audited too, coincidentally, and plus she was under investigation for embezzling and on suspension for an unreported contamination incident. I gave her a little hug, and I closed her cubicle door. I said, 'You probably want to be alone.' She shook her head no.

I said, *(gently)* 'Well ... I want you to be alone.'

*(She slips her hand inside her knapsack and withdraws a bottle of white-out. She begins to white out something on the third document.)*

I went through one difficult period with it all. Made a few calls. From pay phones. But apparently there are strict regulations about what the assessors will or will not discuss with you on the phone. Like, where they live, say. *(malignantly)* Even though they know where you live.

*(She blows on the page to dry the white-out.)*

You're supposed to send the list back in by mail or fax before you come, but I didn't do that. Because I just can't seem to fit my answers into the little 'spaces provided on the form.'

You see, the reason I've deducted all the hair products is because of the mercury vapours in the factory. Which are very drying and a hazard of the job. And if you have long hair and it gets brittle, it breaks off and clogs the filters and then they make you cut your hair short and wear a *(she shudders)* hairnet.

*(She stares at the document for a moment. She shakes her head, shrugs and writes something down, then whites out something else.)*

The reason for the hand creams is the same. Because if your hands get too dry and they get chapped and bleed, they make you put on these thick rubber gloves which slow your productivity. Because any time you spill the mercury? And it falls on the floor and bursts apart into all those shiny, sparkly little bubbles? The best way to pick it up is to go like *(she mimes licking her fingertip and picking up a bead of mercury with it)* ... that.

*(She blows on the white-out. Again, she shakes her head, shrugs and writes something down. Then she stands and walks down to the banker's box, blowing on the white-out.)*

*(Absently)* If I had to wear a hairnet? I would just die.

*(She kneels at the box, puts the first rust-red envelope on the floor, pulls out a second rust-red envelope, blows once more on the third document, then puts it inside the second envelope, which she licks and seals. She picks up the first rust-red envelope and holds it as well.)*

But I don't think I have anything to worry about, really. After all, we live in a just and compassionate society. *(super-affable)* That's what we pay taxes for. And in spite of everything that's been happening to me, I still believe that humans have virtues, and souls, and are basically kind. Sometimes you have to pay for kindness now. More. Like where I used to get my legs waxed? Before they started to garnishee my wages? After my loan? The aesthetician used to hold my hand when she ripped the wax. And maybe it's because I tipped her twenty percent, but just because you're paying doesn't mean they're not nice; it's just a new kind of nice. Like how denim is the new black. I would have tipped her fifty percent to hold my hand if I had to. Which I didn't. It's sort of complicated, but –

I guess that's what I mean by neo-Buddhist more.

*(She licks and seals the first envelope.)*

I lost the official tax receipt for my foster child, so I'm hoping they'll accept her letters as proof of ... that ... as proof ... 'cuz I've just been so super-busy lately, so *(her fingers flutter over her toque)* my mind's a sieve.

*(She puts both documents into the box, then pulls out a third rust-red envelope. She closes the lid of the box and puts down the envelope.)*

Am I hot in here or is it just me?

*(Musical interlude: sad and sweet. A warm spotlight appears by the piano. Pochsy sees it.)*

Um … This next song is dedicated to anyone who's ever had difficulty expanding their concept of existence and has been mystified or terrified by the accuracy of ancient prophecies and troubled by the vagueness of more contemporary visions.

*(She crosses into the spotlight and leans against the piano.)*

It's called 'I've Got the 'I'm Having Difficulty Expanding My Concept of Existence and Am Both Mystified *and* Terrified by the Accuracy of Ancient Prophecies and Troubled by the Vagueness of More Contemporary Visions' Blues.' *(Beat.)* Only it isn't blues. It's way more contemporary than that.

*(She hops up on the piano and, for the first time, notices the bald musician, whose T-shirt's Lead World logo matches hers. She peels off her own T-shirt, revealing a little black tank top beneath.)*

And it goes something like this:

*(She sings 'Buddha.' Melancholy, poppy and very trippy, the song sustains regular corruptions of rhythm and form.)*

> Once upon a different time,
> The world was just and fair.
> Truth and Light went with me,
> I saw Mercy everywhere.
> Now Truth's inconsequential,
> I see darkness in the Light.
> This I saw when I left work last night:

I saw Mercy sitting in a juice bar,
Sipping Silent Spring water with Reason.

*(She speaks)* He's lost weight.

Reason talked about his sadness for the world
While necking with a sixteen-year-old girl.
I went over to their table

*(She speaks)* But it was like I didn't exist.

I guess with all that white light in their eyes
They couldn't see
Me.
Who doesn't need a little girl sometimes?
A beacon in the blight.
But I just wanna ask them,
'When you turn out that light,
What do you dream at night?'

*(Music break. Pochsy looks at the musician, a bit confused. She looks at the audience. She sings.)*

I saw Justice at the fitness centre,

128

Hangin' 'round the scales.

In a terry robe blue as the sky.
But when she took her Ray-Bans off I saw,

Under the makeup,

Rainbow-coloured bruises,
And little stitches 'round her eyes.
She looked like she was twenty,
But I know she's not that young.
She's clearly had a little 'work done.'

She said it was corrective:
She'd been blind,
Now she can see.

Well, I just wanna tell her,
'Honey, I won't judge you
If you don't judge me.'

*(Piano solo. Pochsy looks at the musician, who looks back at her.)*

I saw Moses dining out with Christ.
They shared some wine then bickered 'bout the price.
The price was high, the bottle 33 AD
Jesus said, 'My friend, you split a sea –
Can't you split this with me?'
I went over to their table
'Cuz I knew Jesus, this I know,
And He loves me, but seemed confused.
Well, that's cool; I've got all the friends that
I can use.

They booked Honour on a hit-and-run,
Grace ripped off a screenplay.
Valour's gone to Pakistan
To adopt a kid whose parents blew awa-a-a-ayyy.
I hear Mercy's heading north;
She's selling reconditioned pop machines
To strung-out polar bears,
They're licking cola off the icy be-e-e-each.


Aaaaaahhhhhh ...


Through my thick-lashed eyes
I see a world about to be.
But I won't rush to judge it
'Cuz it's all Greek to me.
I drove home last night and saw
With perfect thick-lashed sight
A dream that's wild and true,
Now, what will I see tonight?
What will I see tonight?


*(Pochsy listens while the song finishes, pulls her Clarity out of her pocket, then says, out of the silence:)*


I'm sorry about what I said earlier. About that old lady. I know I should have more respect for the elderly. It's just that ... when they were young and beautiful?

They had no respect for me.


*(The Musician hits a loud, discordant chord as Pochsy takes a sharp sniff of her Clarity. She hops down off the piano and starts circling the stage. Over the following scene, a discordant, arrhythmic, yet beautiful composition accompanies Pochsy's rant. She sniffs repeatedly from*

*the vial of Clarity – each sniff accompanied by a smash from the piano.)*

They say if you want to know what you were doing in the past, look at your body now, but if you want to know what will happen to you in the future, look at what your mind is doing now.

*(She sniffs.)* In the future, the aging process will be slowed and eventually arrested entirely. The genes that trigger senescence and death will finally be disarmed. *(She sniffs.)* Within our lifetimes, glaucoma, osteoporosis – and even crepe neck – may be things of the past.

*(She sniffs.)* In the future, science will work with our bodies' own natural tendencies toward renewal and regeneration: subdermal implants stimulating the body's own production of collagen, a weekly pill to keep your lips pink as a child's.

*(Music hard out.)*

*(Coltish)* I don't know if I want to have a child, but I do know I want to look like one.

*(She sniffs Clarity. Music back in.)*

But longer lifespans will bring with them, paradoxically, a preoccupation with death and a longing for life beyond this one, and increasingly, people will seek refuge in the realm of spirit for tranquilization.

*(Music out. She stops.)*

Er … *(she corrects herself)* tranquility.

*(Music in.)*

Eventually, suffering and pain will be eradicated as science learns to tap directly and innocuously into the brain's pleasure centres to self-tranquilize and self-stimulate.

*(She shakes the vial – it is nearly empty.)*

In the future, people will be divided not by race, or religion, or even age, but by their ability or inability to partner change.

*(She runs her finger across her gums.)*

We have not been abandoned by our gods: we are being released by them. To form tribes of earthly gods and goddesses, spiritually evolved, unnaturally peaceful, blessed with manifold loves in our lives, young and beautiful ... forever.

Eternal life is within our reach. Infinity is on our minds. And I believe what could be should be. *(She shakes the bottle hard.)* Some might call us monsters. *(Big sucking sniff.)* I say we're only being human.

*(She hisses)* And we are not finished yet!

*(She looks at the empty vial. She stands and hurls it backwards into the void. Music peaks, then stops. Lights snap to nighttime pretty.)*

I got invited to this party a couple weeks ago?

Well, I wasn't actually invited: I was more just kind of surfing around with my scanner? Listening to people's conversations? On their cellphones? While I was driving? And I heard these people talking, who seemed really in tune with what people are starting to articulate about the new century, and they were talking about this party that sounded like it was going to be absolutely unbelievable. So I took down the directions ... and I went.

*(Party lights: sparkly.)*

It was the kind of party where everyone's wearing dark clothing
and nibbling bits of free-range kangaroo sausage and everybody
speaks to each other in a way that's both sexy *and* respectful? I
myself was wearing this – well, it's sort of hard to describe – I was
kind of going for this sort of seventies/eighties/Afro-
Japanese/Mata Hari thing – which you *definitely* need a certain
presence to carry off. *(She giggles and flicks her hair.)*

Anyway, around midnight, all the moms took the babies
upstairs to put them to sleep on top of all the long suede coats on
top of the beds, and the other women we all talked about how
great those women looked, and then *(incredulously)* the men
cleared all the dishes!

Then everybody stepped out into the zen garden, and we all
passed around the 'polite drugs.'

We dangled our feet in the black-bottomed swimming pool,
and people started talking about everything from biotechnology
to the scattered values and goals of an economically driven
culture and ... stuff ...

And I looked around at all the beautiful guests with their
edgy haircuts and their thick-rimmed glasses, and I just wanted
to pinch myself. All I could think was: 'These are exactly the
kinds of friends I have always imagined for myself.' And in that
moment, for just one moment, I really did believe, 'It's okay,
Pochsy. Everything's going to be okay.'

*(Pause.)*

But then at one point, this one girl, the one in the distressed alli-
gator jacket? She started talking about the, um ...

*(Music out. She pauses to think.)*

Oh, what was that? The, um … *(She thinks harder.)* Oh, God! It's famous. *(She racks her mind. Her eyes focus on a point in space.)*
The-e-e-e … Oh! God!

*(She smacks her forehead.)*

The Holocaust!

*(Little sigh of relief.)*

She started talking about the Holocaust.

Now, I was never very good at history; I dunno, I just find it boring. *(She rolls her eyes.)* It just seems like the same things happening over and over and over again!

So, while she was talking about that, I tried to sort of redirect the conversation onto something a little more contemporary, and I started talking about the whole Buddhist thing, you know, cleaving to the *present* moment and all that?

And, like, I don't really care; I mostly just do yoga now, which all the other women did as well, and so I started to tell them all about this new studio, 'cuz everyone is always searching for the perfect class that's not too big 'cuz lately they all just pack them in like sardines, which I think is immoral and completely goes against Buddhist teachings …

*(Pause.)*

But the whole time, the Holocaust girl was just staring at me.

*(Pause.)*

She tossed out some one-liner about 'awakeness' or something, which everybody else laughed at, but which I did not get. Then she smiled right at me, she tilted her head and she said, 'But what about the past?'

*(Pause.)*

And I knew there was a right answer which they all knew, but I was so not into her ideology at that point in time, so I just tilted *my* head, and I said: 'All things are as a river.' That time never stops. 'There *is* no past,' I said. 'There is only the present.'

Well, right then, I felt my first earthquake!

*(Delighted)* It was just one of those little ones, you could barely feel it. But all the birds woke up in the trees, and spidery cracks opened up in the bottom of the pool, and people started joking nervously about the illusion that decadence is indefinitely sustainable – you know, just trying to lighten things up – and the hosts were making reassuring jokes about insurance and that …

*(Pause.)*

But the whole time, the Holocaust girl kept staring at me.

Some of the babies woke up from the coats, so all the moms went upstairs, but the Holocaust girl had no baby (wonder why?) and so she walked around the pool, came over and sat down right beside me out of all the other guests. She put her hand on my leg and she said, 'Then tell me about the future.'

*(Pause.)*

And I knew there was a right answer but I couldn't even imagine a future at all with her hand on my leg and her staring at me like she was the be-all and the end-all of the world, and all I could hear were the babies crying and the birds all freaking up in the trees.

So I looked through my thick-lashed eyes deep into her thick-lashed eyes, I swallowed my tab of 'e' and I just said, *(very still)* 'The future is now, honey. It just hasn't happened yet.'

*(Sound and lighting shift. haunting.)*

I looked deeper in her eyes and told her I had just come there to have fun. I looked deeper still and asked her where she got her jacket. I looked deeper still and asked her what kind of moron she thought I was. She didn't seem to know.

So I got up and went over to the oyster bar, where there was some kind of white-trash scene … which I started …

I don't remember much after that.

I don't even remember driving home.

*(Pause. All lights fade to black over the next moments except a single cold, hard spotlight.)*

But in spite of everything that happened that night, I do still believe that people are basically good at heart. Some are just more 'awake' than others. I want to be awake. I mean, we live but once in this world. How many more vacations is that? How many special vacations?

They say, in, um, *(gently, politely)* Chinese … they say, 'May you live in exciting times.' Which we do. Which is *why* I focus on the *present*.

*(She looks at the rust-red envelope on the lid of the banker's box, lifts the lid carefully and pulls out a daytimer.)*

Which is why I've been using a daytimer lately. It's like a journal, only ... less insane. It reminds me of my appointments and meetings and my dates ... 'n' things. Let's see what it says today: 'Get audited. Go home.' But it's good, see, 'cuz there's a structure there. And once that's in place, my mind is free to be creative within that structure. To imagine and build a beautiful future. *(smartypants)* Which you can only do in the present.

*(Pause.)*

This daytimer was actually made in China *(soft smile)*.

Plus, Angie told me daytimer notes can be helpful in an audit, to support claims. I don't know about you, but for me, if it isn't written down? *(She mimes information flying from her mind.)* Psshhhew!

*(Blackout.)*

*(In the black, Pochsy walks way upstage and leans against the back wall where she is caught in a bright headlight.)*

Last night, after work, I organized my books and records. Then I took them out and put them into the trunk of my car. So I wouldn't forget. Them. Then – I don't know why – I got in my car and I went for a drive downtown. One of those crazy 'fuck it' drives.

*(Rolling driving music. A greenish mist drifts in the air.)*

I drove and drove for miles through this city built for cars. I drove and drove until I was on shaky ground and the asphalt crumbled beneath my tires. I drove until the sky was black and the streetlights all came on *(music out)* – well, not all of them, some of them did but, actually, a lot of them weren't working, so it was pretty dark *(music in)* –

*(Pochsy begins to creep very very slowly along the back wall toward the other side of the stage, where there is another bright headlight.)*

I drove past high schools where skinny, bearded teachers coached midnight soccer games with phantom nets and phantom balls, while the cheerleaders shared glucose meters in the shadows of the stands.

I drove for miles in amongst the heaping dumpsters which leaked garbage juice that ran in streams along the sidewalks and into the streets where cyclists skidded across the rainbow slicks and soared into the sides of Acuras and *(in a German accent)* Volksva-agens.

*(Pause.)*

I've never been in an accident myself *(music out)* – oh!

*(She steps out of the headlights and walks out into the audience in complete blackness. She knocks on the wood of a chair or on the audience floor.)*

Touch wood.

*(She goes back into the headlights.)*

Well, one. But I just caused it; I wasn't in it. There was an ambulance going through an intersection, but I was listening to my music at the time, so I couldn't hear the siren. And anyway, no one got hurt. *(little pause)* Well, the guy in the ambulance was hurt, but that was from a different accident.

But, like, I don't know that after twenty-five million dead you can really call them car 'accidents' any more, I mean, duh – we know they're going to happen. They're more an element. Like weather. Which is why I think no-fault is so good. I don't think anybody should be liable. We all have to drive; I mean, what are you going to do? Stop driving?

*(Pause. She seems to consider this.)*

Where was I?

*(She turns to the musician, who resumes playing.)*

Thank you.

*(She continues to creep along the back wall.)*

I drove and drove back way uptown and past an all-night daycare where sugar-wired toddlers huffed their inhalers and screamed their moms' and/or dads' names into the blackness of the night.

I rocketed through a hospital zone where emergency patients mingled in the foyers sipping Orange Julius and nibbling Mmmmmuffins, tending to each other's cuts and burns. I saw one old man in a wheelchair scream 'CLEAR!' while another patient rubbed paddles over his own chest. And I waved to all the nurses in white dresses, standing on ladders, just … turning back the clocks.

I sped crosstown through twisting streets, my four-wheel independent suspension allowing me to soar over speed bumps and small squirrels without feeling a thing. I hurtled through industrial parks, past the airport, past the army barracks all glowing and cozy in the night. I drove until my engine ran on fumes. I drove into the dawn's early light, and I had never felt so connected. To a car.

*(The headlights begin to flash in slow alternations. Pochsy dances in slow motion.)*

I was not just driving now. I was exploring: the motion of two bodies through the ether, the courtship that never tires, the dance that never ends, the dance that defies gravity's immense hold on us all. Friction's ever-present barriers. Motion. Freedom.

And I was just about to recognize that I was hurtling through an ether that was particular to this and only this light heartbeat in the history of time; and I was just about to recognize that the present is only a random point in the longer flow of time, endless before and endless after; and I was just about to apprehend the wonder of the myriad sea creatures fossilized so deep beneath my tires 200 million years ago; and I was just about to apprehend the magic of the galaxies that were not even there for the first six billion years of time; and I was just about to understand that I was not the be-all or the end-all of this or any other moment in the history of the universe ... but then I drove onto the shoulder, I passed a dozen cars, I heard the screech of tires, and I saw reflected in my rearview mirror ... *(mesmerized)* that silver Infiniti, rolling over, and over, and over into the ditch and I thought, 'Wow. That car *was* built to last.'

*(Hungrily)* I want one.

*(Headlights black out. A dim greenish shaft of light appears in the fog. Pochsy steps into it.)*

When I was very young and I drank from a bottle, everything was about me. My needs, what would make me happy, or at least stop me from crying. Then, as I grew older, it became less about

me. And I fear that it will stay that way *(she whispers)* for the rest
of my life.

*(A hard-edged follow spot hits her from an angle and follows her from
now until the end of the show. Music in full: a driving, urgent cabaret
tune. Pochsy sings 'Only Being Human.' As with 'Buddha,' the song
regularly abandons or mutates its rhythm and form.)*

> Father forgive me, but
> You made my flesh weak,
> You parched my skin,
> Parched my hair,
> Now hear my burning prayer.
> All that I want is a
> Home somewhere far
> Far away from the cold air that's
> Blowing 'round everywhere.
> Stock it with fire logs
> In bright paper packages,
> They burn for hours
> But don't turn to ashes.
> Fill the deep freezer with
> Seedless fruit, boneless meat,
> Farm-fresh sockeye.
> Is that insane or am I
> Only being human?
> Dreaming while I drive
> Of a semi-residential land
> Where two and two make five.

*(Dance break.)*

> Then, on a perfect day,
> Love might just come my way.

He'll rest his head
Beside mine on the three-hundred thread.
Each night we'll thunder home
Through traffic calming zones,
Doff our suede coats,
Kiss the pulse in each other's throats.

Drink from each other's tongues,
Breathe from each other's lungs,
His fingers wet with tears,
Slipped in between my – *(erotic little gasp)* fears.
As he will find,
It quiets my mind.
Soothes me quite painless.

*(Spoken, like an ad:)* Sweet nothings are stainless.

And we'll be
Only being human,
Hear nobody else's cries.
Deep in Semi-Residentia
The future's looking bright.

*(Pochsy dances.)*

Then, with a child or three,
We'll taste infinity.
What does it matter?
We're all mad as hatters, so
Two point five, round it up,
What if eight's not enough?
Scary, this world,
But we would like another girl.

Row row them down the stream.
Waterfalls fill their dreams.
Is it our fault what we
Do accidentally?

*(She does a little pelvic thrust, then shrugs.)*

Or are we
Only being human?
Hear nobody else's babies' cries.
But how can it be wrong
To want to love until we die?

We'll be
Only being human
Beneath an endless sky,
With Baby Be-And-End-All
Swaddled in Arctic fleece – oh my!

*(Pochsy climbs on top of the banker's box. Lights shift into an aberrant version of a prayer state: a horribly bright cold shard pointing straight down.)*

Oh God, release me,
I can't stand this loneliness.

My heart is sore and it's
Beating me to death.
Have You abandoned me or simply set me free?
It's a weird story: though Thine is the glory,
You made it so evil could spring from the jaws of good.
It's not my place to say—

I'll say it anyway:


Looks like You're
Only being human,
But I've forgiven You,
Though You've forsaken me,
Promising five from two and two.
Yeah, You're
Only being human.
You turn Your back on all the little babies' cries,
But I will keep on loving You.

*(She wags a threatening finger at God.)*

As long as I'm alive.


Yeah, You're
Only being human,

Dreaming while you drive,
But I will be your baby lamb,
As long ...
As I'm ...

*(She points her finger at herself.)*

*(Very softly)* Alive.

*(Pochsy tries to fling her long hair over her shoulder, but her hair catches in her nails. She pulls her hand away, and her toque and all her hair come off with it: underneath the wig, she has very short fucked-up black hair, covered with a thick black hairnet. The musician stops playing and watches her. She tries to hide her head. She cannot get the wig back on, so she replaces her toque, and just holds the wig in her arms. She glares at the musician, who resumes playing 'Only Being Human.')*

Every evening in the evening I punch out at nine p.m. I give my voucher to the guy, speed out from the underground, power-lock my crumple-proof doors.

Every evening in the evening I climb up a thousand stairs and sit inside my tiny room and stare out through my window at this city built for cars.

Every evening, far below my window, little children play hockey on the dark twisting street. They do not hear the nearly silent engines but sense them, spin around and cry out 'CA–!'

*(Silence.)*

Every evening I look out across the street and watch as all the lights come on at Mercury Packers and I ponder refraction and the physics of a lime-green sky until the nighttime cools the air above the stacks and rain falls down and strikes against my window where each drop bursts apart into a thousand shiny, sparkly bubbles.

And every evening before I go to sleep I pray that they won't put that little dress at Kinderslut back out on the floor. That I can pay it off. Before the next party. Before the next earthquake. Before my next vacation. So that someday I might find that special someone who will love me.

In the end.

Maybe an accountant. (*She smiles.*) Who is also a fireman.

(*Pochsy lays the wig down on her banker's box and strokes it a few times, with great affection and infinite tenderness. Then she puts it inside the third rust-red envelope, seals it up, drops it into the banker's box, and closes the lid.*

*She takes the box back to the waiting-room chairs, which are now lit only with sickly-green footlights, as well as one special light, which, spectacularly, lights all the garbage spilling across the floor.*

*As Pochsy walks away from the audience, another logo is now visible on the back of her tank top, where her long hair used to fall: it is a cartoon panda bear inside a sparkly pink cartoon heart.*

*She perches on the edge of a chair and adjusts her hat at a jauntier angle. She drapes an arm across the back of her chair and crosses her legs, elegantly.*)

When they give you your appointment, they tell you to put aside a full day.

(*Pause. She gazes off right.*)

And at a certain point, you realize you just have to submit. There's nothing you can do. And there's nothing they cannot do. So you just ... submit.

146

*(Pause.)*

I've been thinking a lot about my foster child lately.

*(She concentrates. Then she says it, calmly, clearly.)*

Azzrajmaibar Zaijan.

*(Big smile.)*

And sometimes I think I might start writing her again. You know, depending on what happens here today. Touch wood.

*(Pochsy's musician knocks on wood. She glances at him, furtively. She pauses.)*

In her other letter, she thanked me for my compassion. She said my monthly contribution of twenty dollars had paid for school-books and milk for all the children in her village and also-o-o-o for-r-r-r ... *(she thinks, remembers and smiles)* a bus.

Then she asked, 'If it is wrong to disparage any single religion, would it be okay to disparage them all?'

*(Pause.)*

I didn't know what to say to that. And I think that's right around when I got so super-busy. But if I were to send her a letter some-time, again, in the future, which who knows? I would just tell her to pray for strength.

And if she couldn't find faith to pray, I'd tell her to just close her eyes and imagine a beautiful future.

And if she couldn't imagine a *beautiful* future, I'd tell her to remember that every day is a day when nothing has to happen, but anything could.

And if she was scared by what could happen, I'd just say …
'Takuna Mahata.' It's from *The Lion King*. It means 'no worries
for the rest of your life.' *(big Chiclet smile)* In African.

I'd say, 'The future is now. It just hasn't happened yet.'

I'd say,

*(A sweet circus-like tune plays. Pochsy sings 'Horribly Beautiful World.')*

> When the bee stings, when the dog bites,
> When the earth quakes in the black night,
> Sing this sweet little song, little girl.
>
> Kitten whiskers, woollen mitts,
> Life's a cosmic magic trick
> And it's a horribly beautiful world.
>
> So, when the wind blows, and the bough breaks,
> Hear the sound the little birds make:
> It's the song of the horribly beautiful world.

*(Bubbles spill from above onto the stage in front of her. She steps into
the falling bubbles, delighted.)*

> I'd say,
>
> If the pail of water spills
> When you tumble down the hill,
> Sing of spoonfuls of sugar, my pet.
>
> Watch the summer snow fall down,
> Kisses for your broken crown,
> Seem's the party's not quite over yet.

148

So, close your eyes and make a wish,
Cross your little fingertips.
Never mind the broken bough,
Look at what your mind's doing now,
And sing the song of the horribly beautiful world.
The morning sun is crystalline ...

*(Pochsy extends her arms up into the bright spotlight, then retracts them, wincing.)*

But nights are cool, the moon's divine.

*(She smiles.)*

And happy little bluebirds still fly around.
What a terribly perfectly horribly beautiful world.

*(She watches the falling bubbles, then picks up her banker's box and steps through them to centre stage. She swoons a little, then puts the box down, then sits down on it and folds her hands in wait. The follow spot narrows in around her, dramatically, until the waiting-room chairs and garbage are invisible.)*

The world has always been a dangerous place. But in spite of everything, I still believe that people are basically good at heart. And that the world is filled with magic.
I have to believe that: I'm getting audited today.
And I have a time card to punch.
And a little dress on layaway.

*(Pause.)*

Oh, well, I guess it's like they say: the only two sure things in this life are taxes and, um ...

*(She giggles softly.)*

I forget the other one.

*(The musician plays a reprise of 'Centre of the Universe,' only slower and way sweeter. Pochsy sings.)*

> I'm calling to you.
> We'll muddle through from nine till ... nein.
> I'll be your Fraulein Frankenstein,
> I'll be your calming calamine,
> I'll be yours if you'll be mine ...

*(She reaches out with both arms to the audience, her little white band-aid gleaming in the now baby-blue light.)*

> I'll be yours if you'll be mine.

*(Pochsy tosses her head and flicks her phantom hair over her shoulder. She realizes that it's not there any more. She smiles sweetly at the audience and laughs, a bit embarrassed. She folds her hands, points her toes, and tilts her face up to the lights. Lights fade to black. Pochsy watches them fade.)*

**The End**

# The Pochsy Songbook

# The Songs

The songs in the Pochsy plays observe rules and obey laws that are quite dissimilar to those of 'normal' musical theatre. Their purpose is, above all, to serve the satirical intentions of the plays: form follows content every time. Most of the melodies are quite simple (even simplistic) tunes that came simultaneously with the words, as I imagine most nursery rhymes and lullabies – and jingles – come together.

Some of the songs lovingly parody popular genres from the thirties to the present: specifically, styles associated with more commercial, escapist forms of entertainment, like romance, music hall cabaret, contemporary pop and tv ads. Some songs don't even begin to attempt a standard form and will often abandon a sung bridge for a spoken one or inexplicably exist as a smattering of lines that don't even really add up to a song at all. Half-rhymes are favoured over full rhymes if ideas are best expressed that way; rhythm will be compromised or abandoned altogether or if the result is more cutting, pointed or humorous.

I have been amazingly fortunate to have found a collaborator, composer Greg Morrison, who has been willing to sacrifice his hard-earned musical vanity in the name of satire. And, in addition to irradiating the songs with intricate scores and his own additional melodies, Greg's live music and sound adds a magnifying element to the stage performances. Through whole systems of aural 'jokes' (from 'iv unit *glissades*' to 'flying penguin calls' to 'hair fling stings'), he has created Pochsy's sonic universe in a way that can expand the plays' emotional impact, while deepening the satire.

Pochsy's songbook is nearly a hundred pages long, so for this book, we have included only first pages of most of the songs. The complete songbook is available through Coach House Books (mail@chbooks.com or 416 979 2217).

# Everything's Falling Apart

# I'll Believe

# Squid Song

# Dark Green Isle

# I'm Too Young to Die

# Funny Little World

# Someone Good Enough For Me

# Oh, baby

# Seasick Fish

# Blue Skies

# Centre of the Universe

# One Clear Purpose

# Bank

Lyrics as they appear in the score:

"In the blackness of the night, / My branch was lit with a thousand lights. / I saw three tellers at their tills..... whisp- pering on their phones. I asked them why they worked so late. They of- fered me new mort- gage rates. I told them I don't own a home, too scared to buy a- lone. I said: Rock me in yo- ur arms. Hold me while I weep. I'm your cli- ent I'm your ba- a- by. Rock me back to sleep. They swiped my card they wiped my eyes, these c- reps in white shirts blue ties. One held me close, one stroked my hair, one asked me for my

# Buddha

# Only Being Human

# Horribly Beautiful World

# Acknowledgements

With gratitude I acknowledge the inspired participation of my collaborators in these plays: John Turner, without whom I would not have made the first move; Michael Kennard, without whom I would not have made the second; Greg Morrison, who has been my road and stage companion; and most especially Sandra Balcovske, without whose patient, intelligent and most valued collaboration these plays would not have made it safely into being.

The following artists were directly involved in the earliest development of these plays. Their contributions are completely and gratefully acknowledged: Michel Charbonneau, Fiona Griffiths, David Hines, Campbell Manning, Sue Morrison, Gary Mulcahey, David Smukler, Ian Wallace.

Very grateful thanks to my editor, Alana Wilcox, for choosing to make this book. Also: Jason McBride and all at Coach House Books.

For their help with this book: Kathleen Oliver, Kevin Brooker, Gary Mulcahey, Greg Tjepkma, Alex Waterhouse-Hayward and Darren O'Donnell.

The Pochsy plays were developed and produced for the stage under the auspices of Pochsy Productions with funding from the Canada Council, the Ontario Arts Council, the Toronto Arts Council and the Laidlaw Foundation. Gratitude as well to Michael A. Hines and Bernice and Colin Hines for their timely and generous support.

Earlier experimental versions of the *Citizen Pochsy* entitled *Pochsy iii* were developed under the auspices of the Edmonton Comedy Arts Festival and Factory Theatre. These one-night/late-night cabarets were executed under the inspired direction of Sandra Balcovske and Ross Manson.

For their help, inspiration, encouragement and contributions: Brad Richmond, Jennifer Wolfe, Rob Gonsalves, Evelyn Datl, Jeff Bradley, Morris Wolfe, Peter Sherk, Sally Cochrane, Christine Buckell, the Turners and Bent Pines, the Team, Carrie Sager, Mia Blackwell, Andrea Lundy, Anne Hines, Diane Flacks, Sandra Shamas, Ed Sahely,

Kathleen Kennedy, Rick Kunst, Natalie Rewa, Melanie Joseph, David Hoekstra, Chris Parsons, Judith McKee, Andrew Macfarlane, Mike Abel, the Fringes and all their volunteers and technicians, the Theatre Resource Centre, the SPACE, Canadian Stage Company, Theatre Passe Muraille, the Second City, Factory Theatre, One Yellow Rabbit Performance Theatre and the High Performance Rodeo, Martin Amis, the Dalai Lama, Alanna Mitchell, Tim Wynveen, The Bible, Revenue Canada, Richard Feren, Paul Anderson, Richard McDowell, Greg Casselman, Shandra Pritchard, Stephen Schroeder, Gavin Shaw, Nadja Ross, Drew Nelson, Elizabeth Macdonald, Scott Macdonald, Julia Winder, Ross Manson and the Office of Tony Ianno.

Margot Hines, Lisa Bernstein, Jennifer Parsons, Suzy Zucker, Kathleen Oliver, Eileen Smith, Tom Diamond, Carol Rosenfeld, Stella Adler, John Towsen, Philippe Gaulier, Richard Pochinko, Gordon Tisdall, James Edmond, Shirley Faessler and Blake Brooker.

# About the Playwright

Karen Hines is an award-winning performer, writer and director and the artistic director of Keep Frozen: Pochsy Productions. Her plays *Pochsy's Lips*, *Oh, baby (Pochsy's Adventures by the Sea)* and *Citizen Pochsy: Head Movements of a Long-Haired Girl* have been presented across Canada and the USA. She is also the writer and co-composer (with Greg Morrison) of the Chalmers- and Dora-nominated musical play *Hello ..., Hello (A Romantic Satire)* which was presented at Toronto's Factory and Tarragon Theatres. Karen is a long-term collaborator with Canadian horror clown duo Mump and Smoot, and has directed all of their shows including *Something, Caged, Ferno, Something Else* and *Flux*. She has appeared extensively in television and film, including leading roles in Ken Finkleman's acclaimed television series *The Newsroom, Foreign Objects* and *Married Life*. She continues to work on stage, in television and around the world.

# About the Collaborators

## Greg Morrison

Greg began working in theatre as musical director for the Second City Touring Company. Composing and musical direction credits include *Pochsy's Lips, Oh, Baby, Citizen Pochsy* and Karen Hines's musical play *Hello ... Hello*, as well as Mump and Smoot's *Something Else* and *Flux*, and (with Lisa Lambert) *The Drowsy Chaperone* (Mirvish Productions). Greg was composer, book writer and producer of his own musical, *The Age of Dorian*. Other credits include *The Muckrakers* (CBC Radio), *Alumnae Cafe* (Tim Sims Playhouse), *The Joe Blow Show* (Comedy Network) and *Slings and Arrows* (Rhombus). His work has received numerous nominations and awards across the country.

## Sandra Balcovske

Sandra graduated from the University of Lethbridge with BA in Philosophy. She moved to Toronto and joined the Second City, where she directed eight Mainstage shows. Sandra has also worked as a director and collaborating writer on a number of original productions, including Linda Griffith's *The Game of Inches, Spiral Woman and the Dirty Theatre*, Karen Hines's *Pochsy's Lips* and *Oh, baby,* Bob Bainborough's *Plastered in Paris* and Lorraine Behnan's *Penguins, Penance and Purgatory*. Sandra has been nominated for numerous Dora Mavor Moore Awards for her direction. She has written extensively for Canadian television and radio, and for four years was Creative Consultant for Second City Canada.

## John Turner

John is co-creator, with Michael Kennard, of the award-winning horror clown duo Mump and Smoot. He attended three universities but was never inspired to finish. He had jobs as a roughneck, orderly, construction worker, frying-pan salesman and bartender. He studied clown, mask and movement with Richard Pochinko, Ian Wallace and Fiona Griffiths, *bouffon* with Philippe Gaulier, physical comedy with John Towsen, and improv comedy at the Second City. With Mump and Smoot he has co-written and performed in *Something, Caged, Ferno, Tense, Something Else* and *Flux*. Directing credits include Tomson Highway's *A Trickster Tale* with the De-ba-jeh-mu-jig Theatre Group. John continues to direct and teach around the world and on his farm on Manitoulin Island.

Typeset in Granjon and printed and bound at the Coach House on
bpNichol Lane, 2004.

Edited by Alana Wilcox
Cover design by Rick/Simon
Cover photo by Gary Mulcahey, courtesy of the photographer
Photographs on pages 3, 8, 16, 24, 26, 30, 31, 36, 37, 41, 42, 45, 50,
     52,. 53, 54, 56, 83 and 150 are by Gary Mulcahey
Photograph on page 21 is by Peter Battistoni
Photos on pages 62 and 74 are by Greg Tjepkema
Photo on page 87 is by Alex Waterhouse-Hayward
Photos on pages 90, 92, 104, 107, 109, 115, 116, 119, 122, 124,
     127, 134, 142 and 143 were shot and captured from video by
     Richard McDowell
Musical scores by Greg Morrison

Coach House Books
401 Huron Street (rear) on bpNichol Lane
Toronto, Ontario
M5S 2G5

416 979 2217
1 800 367 6360

mail@chbooks.com
www.chbooks.com